T0338060

Shakespeare's Reformation

Other Books of Interest from St. Augustine's Press

Nalin Ranasinghe, *The Confessions of Odysseus*

Nalin Ranasinghe, *Socrates and the Gods:*
How to read Plato's Euthyphro, Apology and Crito

Nalin Ranasinghe, *Socrates in the Underworld: On Plato's Gorgias*

Nalin Ranasinghe (editor), *Logos and Eros: Essays Honoring Stanley Rosen*

René Girard, *A Theater of Envy: William Shakespeare*

Jeremy Black, *The Importance of Being Poirot*

Jeremy Black, *In Fielding's Wake*

Joseph Bottum, *The Decline of the Novel*

Rémi Brague, *The Anchors in the Heavens*

Rémi Brague, *Moderately Modern*

Marvin R. O'Connell, *Telling Stories that Matter: Memoirs and Essays*

Josef Pieper, *Traditional Truth, Poetry, Sacrament:*
For My Mother, on her 70th Birthday

Anne Drury Hall, *Where the Muses Still Haunt: The Second Reading*

Alexandre Kojève, *The Concept, Time, and Discourse*

David Lowenthal, *Slave State: Rereading Orwell's 1984*

Gene Fendt, *Camus' Plague: Myth for Our World*

Nathan Lefler, *Tale of a Criminal Mind Gone Good*

John Poch, *God's Poems: The Beauty of Poetry and the Christian Imagination*

Roger Scruton, *The Politics of Culture and Other Essays*

Roger Scruton, *The Meaning of Conservatism: Revised 3rd Edition*

Roger Scruton, *An Intelligent Person's Guide to Modern Culture*

Stanley Rosen, *The Language of Love: An Interpretation of Plato's Phaedrus*

Will Morrisey, *Shakespeare's Politic Comedy*

Will Morrisey, *Herman Melville's Ship of State*

Winston Churchill, *The River War*

Shakespeare's Reformation

Christian Humanism
and the Death of God

Nalin Ranasinghe

Edited by Lee Oser

St. Augustine's Press

South Bend, Indiana

Manufactured in the United States of America.

1 2 3 4 5 6   27 26 25 24 23 22

Library of Congress Control Number: 2022940109

Hardback ISBN: 978-1-58731-817-7
Ebook ISBN: 978-1-58731-799-6

∞ The paper used in this publication meets the minimum
requirements of the American National Standard for Information Sciences –
Permanence of Paper for Printed Materials, ANSI Z39.48-1984.

St. Augustine's Press
www.staugustine.net

TABLE OF CONTENTS

EDITORIAL PREFACE

I have edited this unfinished work by Nalin Ranasinghe in the belief that its author's remarkable genius will excuse, in the minds of genuine humanists, errors and omissions that many professional Shakespeare scholars would find unacceptable. The author, who seems to have had great swaths of Shakespeare by heart, does not distinguish between verse and prose. He makes no references to quartos or folios. Nor does he cite scholars and critics. The draft that I received featured no bibliography and no apparatus at all.

My revisions to the text have been fairly minimal. I have changed the chapter order as I received it only once, by moving the current Chapter Five from its original position, which was between the chapter on *Hamlet* and the chapter on *King John*. I decided to keep the *Hamlet* chapter where I found it, as opposed to arranging the plays chronologically, in the conviction that the *Hamlet* chapter offered a better introduction to the work as a whole. Only in a few cases, by inserting the traditional backslash or slanted virgule (/), have I marked line breaks in verse. Though I have double-checked quotations, I have not tried to establish a standard Shakespeare text for *Shakespeare's Reformation*. As was the case when I assisted with Nalin's *Soul of Socrates* (Cornell UP, 2000), I have made many adjustments and corrections in grammar and syntax; more rarely, I have clarified Nalin's phrasing or substituted a word or a phrase. Never have I tampered with the book's substance, despite my strong disagreement with its thesis. I added the subtitle in order to give the prospective reader a greater sense of what the work is about.

I wish to thank Predrag Cicovacki for his thoughtful assistance in bringing this project to fruition.

L.O.
January 1, 2022
Holden, Massachusetts

CHAPTER ONE
OEDIPUS AT ELSINORE:
HOW *HAMLET* LEGITIMIZES THE RENAISSANCE
WITHOUT LICENSING ITS FURIES

"Who's there? Stand and unfold yourself!" While the very first words of Shakespeare's *Hamlet* invoke the quest for legitimacy, they also pose a question we should ask our text and its protagonist. Though this play about Hamlet is called a tragedy, but may even be a satyr play he stages around and about himself, this does not answer what the sentries, and its audience, ask. What does *The Tragedy of Hamlet* teach, preach or ask of viewers and readers? What is it about Hamlet that has haunted us for 400 years? Lastly, does the play have a meaning? Or is *Hamlet* but a dazzling festival of verbal pyrotechnics and violent passion that signifies nothing?

I will claim that *Hamlet* is more than just a successful revenge play written to entertain the erudite and rivet the rabble. The play has a hidden logic giving its plot mythic force; this adds to *Hamlet's* aura of mystery and gives clues to its deep meaning. While our problem play is ghost piloted by a working stiff to maximize its dramatic power, *Hamlet* also carries about much "dead" weight/dark matter; the chthonic power Hamlet uses/is used by, toxic tradition and thumotic "family values," are what will derail the Renaissance and poison the Christian humanism our Bard offers us. Just as the New Testament is yet constantly stalked by the Old Testament, or *Exodus* by a wish to return to Egypt's fleshpots, furies of the past yet continually wage attritional war on mankind even today.

But my analysis of this play must begin with basic questions. The word *Hamlet*—both a proper name and a noun denoting a village without a church—makes us ask if sublime tragedy is possible in a bastard soul or a place without civilized morals or resident gods. Or will tragedy only visit a secular site, haunted by invisible chthonic powers it denies to its peril? Is it worse to have an established church or nation without friends, villages or colleges? The Bard's defense of decency and common humanity, my basic topic, rests on the real presence and permanent possibility of personal virtue; a just soul is sustained by a subtly benevolent transcendent order: a good beyond being. But what destroyed Hamlet? Are there also dark inner powers that corrupt a soul and rot a city?

If we disregard the earlier tragedy of *Romeo and Juliet*, a comic play that came to a sad end due to accident and misunderstanding rather than character, and did not feature a genuinely tragic hero or heroine, it is clear that *Hamlet* is only Shakespeare's second true tragedy. A second early play with a tragic title, *Richard III*, despite being a great play and a brilliant depiction of the soul of an intemperate evil tyrant, also fails to depict the fall from virtue that characterizes a truly tragic plot; while we see Richard's rise and fall through his own eyes and are almost seduced into congratulating him on his diabolic cleverness, we never feel any real remorse or regret at his comeuppance. Richard is ultimately but a satyr player and divine scourge; he must close the *Henry VI* trilogy. Is Hamlet, full of Mercutio-like quicksilver wit, yet another scourge-satyr? Is he not a symptom or cause of decadence rather than a hapless victim of house plague?

Another play with some claim to being tragic, *Richard II* is not even described as such; the divine language of anointed kingship cannot disguise the fact that Richard II was a nasty young man. The partial self-knowledge Richard gains after his deposition falls far short of the pathos of *Lear*. This was why the tragic Essex rebellion against Elizabeth featured a staging of this play. The audience was not expected to feel any sympathy towards solipsists, anointed or not. There is nothing truly tragic or erotic about Richard II.

Before we look to Hamlet's immediate predecessor, *Julius Caesar*, it is also well worth noting that almost all of the subsequent tragedies, *Othello*, *Lear* and *Antony and Cleopatra*, produce moral or psychic regeneration alongside the death of the hero and or heroine; in other words, even though Christian redemption is not available to the pagan protagonists, the integrity of their souls is somehow restored through the ordeal of sorrow to which it has been subjected. To this extent a tragedy resembles a passion play; even Oedipus undergoes such a change at Colonus. In *Macbeth*, the exception to this rule involving tragedies after *Hamlet*, spiritual rebirth occurs against the backdrop of the struggle against an evil king; Malcolm and Macduff both gain self-knowledge and are mysteriously purified by the extreme losses and terrible grief they endured.

Perhaps this is why Hamlet is so attractive to the modern playgoer and thoughtful reader. Its author does not use a *deus ex machina* to provide cheap solutions or edifying answers to the existential problems he and his prince pose with unmatched eloquence and acute perspicuity; instead our innermost passions and darkest desires are addressed in an authoritative way that conveys both self-knowledge and wholesome ignorance before the sublime. Philosophy is confounded and critical craft is left unmoored by exposure to forces that defy categorization and elude explanation. It is as if the id is addressed by powers beyond the grasp of its superego.

There is also the expectation of hearing an authentic human voice, the freshness of a soul who however briefly resists oppressive social pressures and religious superstitions. Only such a man can slip the surly gravity of tradition and explore the fullest possibilities of humanity. While Bottom the weaver and the Bastard of *King John* blunder past the normal limits of speech and society, only Hamlet is fully rigged to survey these unmapped states and describe to us "with rich eyes and empty hands" what a truly human existence is. But we could be projecting hope on an unworthy hero or redeemer. While Catholicism smothers the soul and Science denies it, Protestantism with its focus on faith and fate cannot explain the forces lurking in the soul or unconscious.

To put it bluntly, we should not be overly willing to ignore the wide difference between rich Renaissance rhetoric and true philosophic-poetic probity; only the latter can really describe the soul's motion and goal. Is it possible that the fine sound and sublime fury of this play should ultimately signify no more than fustian and bombast? Could it be that *Hamlet* is best compared to the Mona Lisa or *Il Trovatore*? The latter work is notorious for combining some of Verdi's best music with his worst plot and most absurd libretto. In short, are we led by the wish to emulate the elite into confusing entertainment with genuine education? Both *A Midsummer Night's Dream* and *King John* suggest how their disguised truths could purge the world's foul body; does *Hamlet* also yield positive insights? What is its meaning? Are the play's many rich images and glorious speeches unified by one great theme? The issue of what the play, or what Hamlet in almost his dying words, is trying to say is distinct from and prior to the matter of whether this claim has been proven adequately. Just as the most heinous actions in Greek tragedy occur off stage, there are things in *Hamlet* that best exert their power via enthymeme, inference or emotion rather than by explicit disclosure in ways best accessible to autistic analytic philosophers and/or algorithmic automata.

I will try to claim that Shakespeare offers an esoteric vindication of the human soul itself, not merely poetry, against the looming backdrop of the Counter-Reformation in Europe and the Puritan perversion of English Anglicanism. Neither the Scholasticism of the former nor the fundamentalism of the latter had any sympathy for the claims of men like Bottom or the Bastard to see beyond the confines of scripture and sacred social structures. While poetry could indulge in metaphysical fantasy, it could not take on the status quo without the assistance of more learned allies; this Shakespeare seems to do by his re-telling of Classical and English history. As disingenuous as Bottom (or Erasmus) in this artful use of ignorance and folly to conceal his serious goals, Shakespeare is thus tying poetry to history and giving us an alternate, if playful, account of Western Civilization.

This chapter argues that *Hamlet* gives us an account of how Prince Hamlet's potent soul, a symbol of all the promise of Erasmus and the Renaissance, was led astray and destroyed by chthonic influences that yet linger in the West's collective unconscious. To support this claim I will explore Shakespeare's own creative consciousness, the list of themes and questions he constantly refines and re-poses in different plays, to decode who Hamlet is and what we are supposed to learn from his downfall. We must identify the dark insidious forces that prevented Hamlet from acting with virtuosity in a situation of the utmost consequence—for himself, his family and his kingdom. Only he had the power to display virtue at a time of transition, one where the pseudo-pieties of a rotten past imperiled the promise of a new age of peace and opportunity for all the people. To fully see his plight, we must turn to another play written by Shakespeare just about a year earlier about an oddly similar man. He too was held hostage by his name, he also had to shed a ruler's blood to redeem his honor, and finally he was also compelled by false necessity to indirectly sacrifice the freedom of his own people and bring about the deaths of those he loved. Just as Caesar had his Brutus, Claudius had his Hamlet; we could learn from these rare examples of virtue destroyed by its self-consciousness.

4

The play *Julius Caesar* could just as easily be called the tragedy of Brutus. While its title character dies in the third act, the remainder of the play discusses his inheritance; it could be said with justice that—like Gaul—this too is divided into three parts. While the play's Mark Antony receives the erotic aspect of Julius, Octavius eventually inherits the title of Caesar, and the dictator's reputed love child, Brutus, is left with his love of honor. The play makes it quite clear that honor is not to be identified with ambition; indeed it is a sign of decadent times when the two terms are found to be in a disjunctive relationship. But what makes the "sterner stuff" of honor readily concede the prow to ambition? How could it be a quality possessed by both Caesar and Brutus' uncle, Julius' deadly enemy Cato? Shakespeare's play seems to suggest that his majestic but moribund Caesar, a man who manifestly suffers from the "falling sickness," seemed to think of himself in the third person. While this could well be the goal of one whose very name was turned into an imperial title, honor as understood by Brutus and Cato somehow combines intense self-consciousness with the burning desire to be thought of as being more constant than the Northern Star. Cato's angry refusal of Caesar's clemency and contemplation of his own entrails in death, his daughter's self-mutilating demonstration of her stoic qualities to her husband and cousin Brutus, and the latter's own efforts to display his indifference towards news of her death, all seem to protest too much; perhaps the last word on Stoicism was spoken by the soon to be deified Augustus, almost sixty years later, when he asked those around his imperial deathbed if he had played his part well. This suggests that Cato had triumphed over Caesar to the extent of convincing his old enemy that posthumous honor meant more than the realization of earthly ambition. Young Caesar, who wept in envy of Alexander's deeds, would belatedly see, at his own triumph, how flat, stale and unprofitable all of Pompey's feats were.

Cassius tempts Brutus into leading the conspiracy against Caesar, the man who loved him most, by appealing to his honor: He must choose between his true father and his reputed ancestor. Cassius, the true originator of the conspiracy, greatly envied the preference his youthful and estranged brother-in-law received from Caesar. A self-proclaimed Epicurean (one believing that gods are indifferent to human affairs), Cassius shrewdly saw that Brutus' care for his reputation for honor was his one weakness. In short, though superior to those rich Roman oligarchs who hypocritically praised honor even as they commoditized it, Brutus overtly values honor above intrinsic virtue. His loudly professed Stoicism refutes itself; he cannot pride himself on his self-knowledge; his weakness is in his having the name of a distant if not mythic ancestor: Lucius Junius Brutus, Tarquin's nephew and the founder of the Republic, a man who slew his own sons when they plotted against Rome. Having renounced the name of his adopted father, taken the side of Pompey, the killer of his legal father, against Caesar and then having been pardoned by him, Brutus is now required by sacred honor to kill his reputed father. Yet strikingly the play never mentions what Plutarch's readers would have known: that Brutus' mother was Caesar's mistress for many years. Thus, while *Julius Caesar* seems emotionally self-sufficient, Plutarch's unsettling revelations haunt Brutus' stoic play and the fine eulogies of Antony and Augustus.

We find that Brutus feels honor bound to fight Caesar's ambition. This or his renowned liberality would have led the dictator to grant recognition and benefits to the urban poor. But it would further oppose him to the economic and political interests of the oligarchs and senators whom he had just triumphed over. Caesar made it overtly clear that he no longer needed the approval and respect of the very people Brutus' honor depended on. He and he alone could have been the King of Rome. So, just for embodying this mere possibility, he had to die. A just king is ever a tyrant in the eyes of the aristocrats, for he must displace them to recognize the potential for virtue in the common people. The aristocrats' claim to rule and riches depends on a sacred and invisible line drawn between the few and the many. They believed that the republic or public space could not be shared with the many. For this they killed Caesar, the one man whose *eros* could have brought the many within the pale of the polity. In revenge, Antony unleashed the many *qua* mob on them. While he could not "civilize" the many, Antony felt compelled by his love of Caesar to fight his enemies; this necessarily had tragic results for himself. Only Augustus was able to "solve" the problem. He did so by politically enslaving both the few and the many. We also note that while both Julius and Jesus seemed to be on the side of the many, Caesar-ism and Roman Christianity turned their erotic spirit into oppressive ideologies.

While revenge and honor blind Antony and Brutus from seeing the good of the common people, Octavius conveniently sees his hypocritical hegemony as its embodiment. The vacuum created by the end of the

Republic is filled by the divinized family of Augustus and Livia; as a result, other rich families can justify themselves by imitation of this holy family. When these family values fully eroded Rome's social fabric, otherworldly religion returned as the force binding the depoliticized whole together. This process culminates in the Emperor Constantine's embrace of Christianity as the best faith to hold his empire together. Soon after, Augustine's doctrines of original sin and just war gave rhetorical justification for Church and Emperor to rule over sinful mankind for another millennium.

Yet even though the idea of original sin is both false and pernicious, its origins—which have to do with the very real and not unjustified fear of the mob—go back further, into Greek tragedy. We must see what is dimly recollected and darkly reflected in the anger of Dionysus and the Furies' rage. And then we must study Hamlet's Greek precedents: Telemachus, Orestes, but most vitally Oedipus, are all precursors of the Danish Prince.

Just as a hamlet is a town without a church, we're now either moving back to pre-Christian times or forward, with the help of Renaissance humanism, to an age of literal "re-formation" where the West's classical and Biblical origins may be recovered and unified for the future. But it could also be the age of a new literalism, one where the Old Testament's worst images would be grafted on to Roman thumotic imperialism, turned into commodity and given to all by this brave new wisdom; the axiomatic methods of modern science would be used to build draconian thought castles while their rulers, godless and the god-intoxicated, sought to wrest all of the power of the old god and the old church to better serve his or their own greater glory. The literal meaning of Elsinore, as Shakespeare chose to spell the Danish "Helsinger," is something like older-god.

In both *Agamemnon* and *Thyestes*, Seneca depicts a condemned shade from Hades returning to visit evil upon our world. Furthermore in each case the ghost carries out his mission in and through his familial home and bloodline. While in Seneca's *Agamemnon* we see Thyestes infect Aegisthus, his son born of incest with his own daughter, with a furious murderous hatred towards his cousin Agamemnon that results in Aegisthus seducing Agamemnon's wife and then convincing her to kill him, he does so because Tantalus had earlier caused his grandson Atreus to kill the sons of his brother Thyestes before serving them up in a dish so their father could unwittingly dine on the flesh of his children. This latter story is recounted in Seneca's tragedy *Thyestes*. In contrast to the *Agamemnon,* where Thyestes' deed is neither depicted nor explained, the *Thyestes* actually begins with Tantalus lamenting his lot and describing how he has been forcibly brought out of his eternal torture in Tartarus to infect Atreus with this ultimate hatred. It is striking that his agency, however coopted, is needed to bring this evil on his house.

The unidentified fury that forced Tantalus out of Hades will not allow the notorious malefactor's preference to suffer worse torments in the realm of oblivion and sorrow. Part of his punishment is in seeing *and desiring to see* how his sin continues to live on in his progeny; worse, Tantalus himself must be the very means by which Atreus will perform an atrocity against his brother that dwarfs the sins of his grandfather. Instead of being endlessly tantalized by the tree laden with fruit he cannot reach, Tantalus is now forced by self-identity, fate and fury to reach out of Hades to corrupt and rot the branches of his blasted family tree. Moreover, only the worst aspect of his soul is allowed to pollinate his progeny; only "the evil that men do lives after them." We recall that Kronos, his grandfather, also tried to eat his children. Only Zeus escaped this fate.

This is consistent with Plato's demand in *Gorgias* that the irredeemable must be shown in their torment by poets so others may learn not to emulate their ways; Seneca makes Tantalus reach from the grave to make this point. The stoic satisfactions of Camus' Sisyphus are not for him. He is tortured: both in Hades and the human present. Here his mental torture comes from being in a never-ending cycle of first wanting and tempting his descendants to be like him (as every ancestor would) and then feeling infinite guilt in their misery and self-hatred. The fury resurrects and incarnates Tantalus' eternal thumos: his hubristic wish to be himself and eternally assert himself by his unique desires. We can learn much about Hamlet's ghost from Seneca. As with Tantalus, the obsessive desire to prove descent or paternity leads to the most awful crimes. We may also dimly discern a common theme of murderous rivalry between two brothers over one woman that ties Hamlet to the tragedies of Seneca. What use we are to make of it is unclear.

Act I scene 2 jumps back in time to a dystopian version of the *Odyssey.* Hamlet makes his first appearance playing Telemachus after the marriage of lusty Penelope to slimy Eupeithes after the death of Odysseus has been

8

confirmed but not explained. It is striking, if not remarked upon, that the old king's death is not mourned very much. Perhaps, just as Odysseus was silently cursed for losing all his men, Hamlet Sr. was also better known for raiding and killing rather than loving his wife and kingdom. Like Telemachus, Hamlet is more concerned with the tarnished chastity of his mother and his loss of standing than the good of the kingdom. These hidden causes lie at the root of his distemper, even though the heavy drinking that goes with the wooing and wedding of this new Penelope to her suitor gives him ample overt cause for displeasure. Being "dumped" by Ophelia soon after this posthumous rejection only adds to his grief.

On finally meeting with the prince, the ghost, who had earlier fled like Christ's betrayer Peter when a cock crew, claims to be his father's spirit in purgatory. But this reference to Catholic doctrine is also consistent with the ghost being from hell if, like Tantalus, his goal is to deceive by false doctrine, spread sedition and do evil. Protestant playgoers and Seneca's readers would see a ghost's return to our world as being by hell's power. It is hard to see how a penitent in purgatory would return to urge murder. Or, to use Solomon's wisdom, no true father would give his son so wicked a task. The ghost has no words of love for Hamlet and the prince has no happy memories of times with him. We note that all his praise of the old king is rhetorical.

It is clearly of great importance to the ghost that only Hamlet should avenge his murder. This is of equal importance to Hamlet since his designation as avenger amounts to a legitimation of sorts; however privately, Hamlet is anointed in blood as Hamlet's heir. The ghost joins Hamlet in requiring that his companions swear thrice (just as Peter did falsely) by their prince's sword, a suggestively pagan vow (despite the fashion for cruciform hilts), not to disclose anything of what had passed that night. But since Jesus told his followers not to swear, and since this oath also echoes Jesus' warning to Peter that those who lived by the sword would die by it, we are entitled to ask whether the ghost is from purgatory, as he claims, or hell? Horatio and Marcellus do not know the content of the ghost's communication to Hamlet; knowledge of the murderous task he was set would only make them more suspicious.

We also observe that the main effect of the poison given aurally by the serpent-brother is to turn his victim into a scaled and venomous thing like itself; it seems too that Hamlet is also rendered unfeeling and venomous by this ugly tale being poured into his ear. We recall that, like the ghost, he too paces Elsinore Castle for many long hours. The tale's aural nature takes added meaning when we see how Claudius responds to Hamlet's "Mousetrap"—its content is not given (*qua* picture) to eyes but to ears. In short, the ghost's tale must be taken symbolically, not *seen* as a literal account. This is how the serpent Claudius soon poisons Laertes with the hope of revenge.

This context gives us a little bit more to go on. Shakespeare often deals with the theme of a king who is just too good or bookish to attend to his duties as a ruler; Prospero is a prime example of this. In this case the old ruler's domestic inadequacies are implicitly added to the charge sheet by our back story; we recall the ease and alacrity with which Denmark accepts its new ruler—albeit to absent Hamlet's shock. King Hamlet is like that other pirate: Odysseus. Even if an heir is provided, the hero king's martial virtue has done his wife, family and people little benefit. In the Bard's depiction of these cases it is the king's brother who's left holding the baby or tending to the daily business of rule. *As You Like It* and *The Tempest* are early and late discussions by the Bard of this dilemma; even *King John*, as we shall see, qualifies under closer scrutiny. It matters little that the heir is hypnotized by troubadour's tales of Othello's noble deeds. In short, *pace* Augustine, sacred, heroic or rhetorical virtues are useless when severed from the moral virtues that hold a city together. King Hamlet and Hamlet, the secret prince of thinking, resemble Richard I and Richard II. Both these latter were very bad kings. In addition it seems that King Hamlet was not a loving husband or father; it is only with familiarity and neglect that quotidian virtues are valued. Cold virtues give out brilliant light without heat.

The *leitmotif* of strife between two brothers is far older than Shakespeare. *Genesis* is replete with stories of sibling strife and reconciliation. But it is Attic tragedy that conveys accounts of how these rivalries last over generations and turn both secret and sacred. Tragedy's care for the city, hospitality and speech requires that the powers of patriarchy and energies of fertility be eroticized; but it also demands disclosure of darker values by which the deceased doom their descendants. The awful words of Aeschylus' *Libation Bearers* "the dead are killing the living!" must be taken very seriously. In short, we must go beyond mere horror to try to grasp what it is about the uncanny that confers menace and meaning in equal measure. Our play's hidden power may come from this very origin.

At one level, the source of *Hamlet's* power is Seneca's tragedy. While Shakespeare has an uncanny ability to channel the power of Greek tragedy, in a way that illustrates the very point I am trying to make, his main acquaintance is with these Roman tragedies. In a sense, this is appropriate. Elizabethan concerns with family, trade and property were more Roman than Greek, but study of Seneca may show how creepy chthonic values, clad in concrete Roman overcoats, were set at the base of an English culture that rejected the Church and yet tried to preserve the Latin tongue, Roman ritual, Classical rhetoric and oligarchic values by using words like "catholic" and "humanism." In fact, we have just listed the substance of Hamlet's humanistic education at Wittenberg; yet the town that educated Luther is also said to host Faust and Mephistopheles.

Fraternal strife may be said to be the beginning of a city. Brother kills brother and then invites strangers and outlaws in to protect him from blood revenge. Yet the bones of the dead brother remain in some chthonic form—at the base of the city and in the blood of his killer. This same man, the founder of the city, uses up tremendous psychic energy in suppressing all memory of his crime. In Freudian terms, he would sublimate or even divinize the basis of his patriarchal power. Or, otherwise put, he has returned to his own mother's womb to exercise a father's right to expose and expel his degenerate sibling. This primordially Oedipal act is the ultimate sacrilege against time, nature and plurality.

Despite progress, Abel's voice still appeals to the older gods of genesis and generation. They too, like Gaia, were suppressed for city and civilization. But the primal rights of the innocent victim, invoked by Job's wife when she urged her tortured spouse to "curse god and die," cry out to high heaven. The ontological status of a simple word of truth, more sacred to the angry theatrical display of Dionysius than to the repressive rituals of Rome, or seen in the power exerted by Solzhenitsyn to storm Stalin's Soviet empire, is a force to be counted—for good or evil. Prodigal truth, if welcomed, can bring great blessings on a home; but if denied, takes a blindly furious form to divide a house against itself. Made mad by scorn, rejection and neglect, exiled truth now visits pitiless sanctions on its own household. This is the tale of Hamlet and his madness but it also gestures behind itself.

Regarding sibling rivalry, Shakespeare's source texts are clearly Seneca's *Agamemnon* and *Tantalus*. These two plays show how adolescent strife is passed down through the generations as a festering fury; this thumotic force offers cheap identity through eternal enmity and promises life beyond the grave. As noted, *Tantalus* focuses on the rivalry between Atreus and Thyestes; it has one brother seducing the other's wife in revenge for his usurpation of rulership. It ends with Tantalus, their ancestral fury, inspiring Atreus to feed Thyestes the flesh of his own children. It should be clear that *Hamlet*, as we have interpreted it, features a similar rivalry between the brothers Hamlet and Claudius; Hamlet wins the crown and the girl but then Claudius wins the girl, kills his brother and gets the crown. Hamlet retaliates by returning in ghostly form and asking his son to kill his brother. But is this revenge fiendish enough? Does it reach the bloody standard *Tantalus* set? Shakespeare has already written *Titus Andronicus*—a gruesome tragedy where its eponymous hero serves the flesh of his daughter's rapists to their evil mother. We must explain the ghost's secrecy and reveal what is so terrible about his vengeance.

Just as *Troilus and Cressida* will show Shakespeare go head to head against Homer and Chaucer, I argue that *Hamlet* is Shakespeare's version of the most famous Greek tragedy of all: *Oedipus Rex*. Rifely riddled with riddles worthy of the Sphinx itself, the play only makes sense to us if we place Seneca's *Oedipus* beside his *Thyestes* and *Agamemnon*. This completes the tragic triptych against which *Hamlet* must be staged.

Although Seneca's *Oedipus* is hardly one of his best plays, this work provides several valuable hints as to how *Hamlet* could be interpreted. Laius' fear, followed by hostility towards his son, is one parallel that sheds light on our puzzle play. A second similarity appears when we see Oedipus' mad obsession with finding the truth. While Seneca's hero is dedicated to seeking the good of his people, something Hamlet seems to care very little about, both characters cannot emulate Jocasta and Gertrude respectively and leave well alone. Hamlet cannot settle lazily in the role of crown prince that he has done very little to earn or deserve. Something rotten within both men demands its objective correlate. The third parallel can be drawn between Claudius and Creon. Both royal uncles are regarded with intense hostility by the nephews despite the benevolence that the older men show towards the younger. This same prejudice is the origin of their downfall. The last likeliness we note is the extreme respect both men show their fathers. Hamlet has sworn to obey the ghost and Oedipus will do anything to avoid killing his supposed sire. Ironically it is this very desire, coupled with Oedipus' quest for oracular knowledge and Hamlet's turn to the ghost, that brings disaster upon their kingdoms.

This long list of parallels and similarities between *Oedipus* and *Hamlet*, added to Shakespeare's demonstrated reliance on Seneca's *Tantalus* and *Agamemnon* to give esoteric ground for *Hamlet*, lead us to seek even deeper affinities between the two equally puzzling masterworks. What happens when we use what we have already found in *Tantalus* and *Agamemnon*, add *Oedipus* and then turn towards *Hamlet*? Bluntly put, what meaning emerges when we read *Hamlet* as Shakespeare's *Oedipus*?

Both plays begin in times of crisis and confusion. In each case a king has died and been replaced as the queen's spouse by one who is not his son. Also, while Thebes is under the grip of the plague, what is rotten in Denmark is most evidently a looming war with Norway but also signified by the old king's ghost. We find later that the plague in Thebes has also been brought on by the rage of murdered Laius—its former ruler. Each spirit will voice outrage that the true cause of his violent death has not been investigated. And worse, the very jointress on whom the realm is conferred has "joined" with a polluted mate.

***

All these things provide ample ground for suspicion that Hamlet is not the king's son. But both King Hamlet and his Queen have good reason for concealing this from the Prince, each other, and Denmark, since Hamlet's virility and capacity to rule (along with Gertrude's chastity) would be called into question. We receive further indirect support for this claim from *Oedipus*; Hamlet would indeed bring about his father's death if Claudius, and he's the best candidate suggested by the play, fathered Gertrude's baby. And even though she does not commit incest with Hamlet, Gertrude would surely have been horrified to know that her lover and husband Claudius has cold-bloodedly tried to kill his son Hamlet. This result would have suited the ghost, who would also have derived much pleasure from seeing his treacherous brother dispatched by his own bastard son; as in the case of Oedipus'

Tantalus, the penalty for seducing a brother's wife must exceed the shame incurred by being cuckolded. The furies exact and exceed *lex talionis*.

While in the case of Thyestes, Atreus finds pleasure in making his brother unknowingly consume his own children, here (if my guess is correct) the ghost has made Hamlet kill Claudius, his own father, for the crimes of adultery and incest against King Hamlet. But Prince Hamlet does not know that he is the unwitting agent of the ghost's heinous revenge against his own parents; neither Oedipus nor Hamlet can see until it is too late that they have inflicted terrible punishments on their own fathers; one that will haunt each mother's last living moment. The broken quasi-families are finally brought together and united in terror, grief and shame by these ultimate acts of pollution. While the terrible price paid by Oedipus settles a long deferred fine imposed on Laius for his abduction and rape of Chrysippus, *Hamlet* serves as an object lesson against the sin of succumbing to the furies of revenge. The tragedies of Oedipus and Hamlet warn us that the furies can disguise themselves as virtues, justice and piety respectively here, when they pollute human souls and intellects to make us righteously perform acts of great evil.

The furies lurk at the very root of thumotic identity; this is how Oedipus and Hamlet are seduced by their sibilant siren song; that is why they cannot be sublimated or defeated unless self-knowledge replaces the generic rage-identity divinized ancestral piety gives.

We began with a tale told by a ghost, a male mail-clad dragon, of poison poured into his ear that caused his death. Yet the serpent's turgid tail also has a procreating potency of its own. Lashing out beyond the grave, it turns an impotent pirate's biological nephew into his posthumous son and so launches a deadly raid on its own origins and offspring. While this chapter will mostly explore the perplexing issues surrounding Hamlet's claims to legitimacy, we must never forget that this vengeful and sin-ridden spirit is not a legitimate representative of the old king's soul.

***

When Hamlet asks the players to recite a fragment of melodrama about the fall of Troy, which he begins and then watches to his satisfaction, the prince reveals a great deal about his own feelings towards his mother and motherland. While the actor's eyes fill with tears as he recounts terrible things, the unhappy prince himself is invigorated by this lurid account. Clearly identifying with Pyrrhus, the vicious son of dead Achilles who slaughtered aged Priam as his wife Hecuba watched helplessly, rapt Hamlet derives great pleasure from the anguish of Troy's "mobled" queen and the terrible fire consuming Troy that parallels the wanton slaughtering of its king. There is an overt connection here with poetic Nero and the artistic pleasure he took from the burning of Rome. The literally pyrrhic victory Hamlet proposes to win over Denmark itself is clearly signaled to us here.

When the players depart leaving Hamlet alone, he upbraids himself for failing to muster the emotion a mere actor was able to produce at this totally imagined spectacle. Yet we must note that while the player felt sorrow at the fall of doomed Troy and aged Priam, Hamlet himself is completely on the side of Pyrrhus. It is to summon up the evidence to justify his playing this Nero-like role that he deploys his "Mousetrap" and tries to "catch the conscience" of Claudius. In short, we cannot forget that Hamlet does this all so as to stifle his own conscience and attune himself to a state of psychopathic rage. Though Hamlet is as preternaturally skilled as Richard III in making us see through his eyes, here he momentarily drops his guard to reveal his febrile soul. The theatrical trap he seeks to use on Claudius also shows Hamlet's tyrannical poet-soul. But this passion to avenge his father does not naturally well up from his nature; it comes from a wish for legitimacy and need for a father. This is why he envies Laertes and Fortinbras. They have natural passion and martial skill but he has "a version" of Claudius' intellect. The duel Hamlet fights with Claudius for the throne is a mad game of mirrors and mousetraps.

In his soliloquy, Hamlet is acting out the nihilistic side of his soul for an audience. His "fury" is concealed. This is fortunate for him since we now know the king to be a criminal. The proof of Hamlet's play-acting is in his calling death "an undiscovered country" from which none return. Regardless of how honest the ghost is, he has returned from there; even if he is not whom he claims to be, he is from that uncharted domain. For Hamlet "the something after death" is more than the mere abstract possibility his soliloquy turns it into. This is all to convince Claudius and Polonius that he is suicidal but not regicidal. This is also why he is so hard on Ophelia. He knows that she is pretending to be alone, but she does not see that he is aware of the deception and using his words accordingly. Hamlet is truly angered when she says that her father is at home. This is the lie direct. His response shows that while he still has feelings for her, he also finds her beauty or seeming to be the means by which her honesty or reality is corrupted; the world is such that non-being, desire for what we lack, or are not and desire, i.e. falsity, always has an edge over the state of being all aspire towards; we end up ruined by this wish for pure being. Ophelia's virtue leads her to become whatever Polonius wants her to be, denies her soul and exiles her from truth and honesty. But is Hamlet any better? Is this why he is so angry? Isn't he as anxious to obey the ghost? Is evil radical and ontological or is it but falsely divinized piety? Is it the will of angry dead men clawing out of their tombs for honor or does it have more to do with alienated young men, reaching desperately into the grave for light, legitimacy or love?

Hamlet's de-nun-ciation, his diatribe against giving birth or becoming, in praise of bald or brazen nunnery, must be seen as rhetorical madness but it also hides a grain of truth. To him the condition of crawling continually between heaven and earth, the position of the poet, is also part of the very punishment Tantalus must endure; it would be easier to be a wretched nun, an abject spiritual worm crawling on earth, or otherwise be either a whore hid in a nunnery or a sinner suffering pain eternally underground. All that flattens the soul is natural and good; works that madden, flatter or lift it hopefully upward are evil.

Is Hamlet/Lucianus God's vengeful cherub with a fiery sword, or Lucifer that shining and mercurial light-bearer? Either way, he envies any love, and hates all mortal frailty. When Hamlet proceeds with his intent to "wring" his mother's heart, he accuses her of an act he will not name that mars marriage, destroys law, addles religion, and even hastens the apocalypse. When Gertrude keeps asking that he name this deed, she is shown two images representing the choice she made between his father and uncle. The old king is given every virtue, based and allegorized on his appearance in the one, while Claudius is unmercifully laden with vices that curiously do not derive from his picture. Instead the prince likens Claudius to "a mildewed ear blasting his wholesome brother." While one evident flaw with this comparison is that it shows men thirty years apart in age, Hamlet himself having noted that miniatures of Claudius had begun to be made after his crowning, the real issue is the heretical choice she is accused of having made of lust over love. It seems that Hamlet here echoes the ghost's claim that "lust, though to a radiant angel linked, will sate itself in a celestial bed, and prey on garbage." But does this mean that the old king was a sexless garden angel? How was this cherub of justice conceived by him? Or could we speculate that Hamlet was spawned in a garbage pit, a smoking Gehenna?

This motif of the two pictures thus explains much about Hamlet's tirade. Ignoring the corpse in the room and even passing over his last obsession, the late king's murder, for now maybe he cannot condemn cold homicide any more, this young Wittenberg Augustinian is single-mindedly focused on the evil of sexual desire. He equates adult love with lust ("for at your age the ... blood is tame, it's humble") and even suggests that rational love ("when reason panders will") between the middle-aged is scandalous and refutes the virtues of shame and chastity. In short, while it's better to marry than to burn, all adult desire is immoral. We recall how he earlier told Ophelia: "We will have no more marriage. Those that are married already, all but one, shall live; the rest shall keep as they are. To a nunnery go." Hamlet then sounded like just St. Paul predicting the imminent apocalypse. But is Hamlet too among the prophets? Or is this a case of a fury quoting scripture? Fanatic fundamentalism and fiendish fury seem to bend back to a common origin.

The nameless gravedigger is perhaps the most likeable character in this play. He is also a Falstaff figure in revealing to his Prince the folly of glory and the glory of folly. Acting in his capacity as a sexton, one of the old church's minor offices, this holy gravedigger duly baptizes Hamlet in the earth and reveals, in this valley of the bones and place of the skull, the absurdity of posthumous striving after power and immortality. Nothing of man survives nine years in the soil. Symbolically, temporarily, Hamlet's consciousness is purged of unwholesome fiery spiritedness, the original sinful legacy he inherited from his "father" but his conscience, marked with fury and guilt, may already be past rehabilitation. The sexton replaces the only man who brought lonely Hamlet genuine happiness: Yorick. The long dead jester (who has the name of the original Gertrude's father and thus stands in for Hamlet's grandfather) is fondly remembered by the prince for "his infinite jest and excellent fancy." He is the origin of the bitter wit Hamlet has internalized.

The gravedigger even reminds Hamlet of the significance of a fact he had either ignored or misread: He was born on the very day his father bested Fortinbras. King Hamlet valued honor and killing above being at his heir's birth. He'd risk his son being born an orphan for glory's sake. The pattern seems to persist posthumously. Whether or not Hamlet is his son, he's required to kill and die for the name and honor of his "father." Hamlet is emancipated from the burden of being King Hamlet's unloved son by this recognition. His slaying and mutilation of Polonius, not to mention the matter of Rosencrantz and Guildenstern, have for better or worse forged his own identity. He will recall that it was Yorick who bore him on his back. Though Hamlet can now be reborn as a bastard, a soiled son of a bitch in the graveyard, he yet has sins and troubles of his own to atone for. They will weigh him down when Ophelia's cortege and her angry brother appear, courtesy of Claudius.

Stepping back a bit, before the final bloodbath, we might reflect on the state of (the) play. We see Hamlet, likely the son of Claudius, but so anxious to kill the king and prove his legitimate descent from someone who never cared for him, that he would risk both his life and his assured succession to the throne to kill someone who could be his father. Likewise, Claudius is plotting to murder someone who is his heir and probably his son, in order to legitimize his crown, his marriage to his wife (who will hate him for killing her son), and his power over an unstable realm. Since, most likely, Laertes will try to kill him next when he finds the truth about Ophelia, Claudius must then scheme to have him killed too. Is it worth it? And we have Laertes, so anxious to prove his credentials as good son that he entrusts his fate to a crooked king who will try to kill him after he does his dirty work.

These badly mimed struggles for legitimacy have left all the principals, including the queen, full of self-loathing. They doubt themselves and suspect each other; there is not one completely honest friendship in existence by the end of this tragedy. Worse yet, by selfishly looking towards non-living thumotic criteria (depicted by the sexton's bones) for legitimacy, they betray their own souls and the common good. Denmark is lost to young Fortinbras, a third young thug trying to redeem his dead disgraced father by his deeds.

Even King Hamlet suffers though his posthumous fury; his legacy is lost since the mad lust for revenge so moves his namesake that he'd even betray Denmark to satisfy it. The dead man's virtues are inverted in his afterlife and set up as absurd standards of manly virility he himself could not follow. And any reformation of old morality, however wise, will be denounced as sinful deviation from sacred tradition by the god-fearing. No one gets to the father except through it.

This eternal impasse leads to cynicism and hypocrisy, even today. Blind worship of a single way of virtue sanctified by ancestral prescription stifles the potential of the souls within a polity, and denies the humanity of all outside it. So instead of a true republic, where humans bring the best out of each other, they live in oligarchies, warped by the imagined virtue of angry old men. Only a real republic can escape these toxic traditions to recollect true archetypal virtues. This is what the Renaissance was meant to be about, but as *Hamlet* reveals, the Reformation and Counter-Reformation mobilized many forms of necrophilia; ghosts or furies of highly dubious legitimacy rose from a sacred or idealized past to meet this threat.

Even if Hamlet himself did not grasp this double-business to which he was bound, and his education at Wittenberg would certainly have given him a better appreciation of it than most, his heart, as he himself admits, was sickened by it. This is perhaps the best reason he is so fatalistic concerning the outcome of the duel: "If it be now, 'tis not to come."

Before the duel, told by Horatio that he would lose, even at the odds, Hamlet admits to misgivings "as would perhaps trouble a woman" but rejects Horatio's advice to obey his mind when it dislikes something. As resigned as Brutus, he defies augury like Caesar. It is ironic that while Brutus unwittingly contributed to Caesar's apotheosis by denying him the crown, Hamlet destroyed his namesake's kingdom by his mad efforts to divinize him.

When Fortinbras and the Ambassadors arrive they exclaim in wonder, but are only told by Horatio to end their search if they seek "woe or wonder." No effort is made to identify the dead to Fortinbras. But how does he know Hamlet? Where did they meet? When the First Ambassador reports the death of Rosencrantz and Guildenstern and asks who will thank him for this report, bold Horatio replies that the king did not command it. He asks that all four bodies be set on a stage so he can "speak to the yet unknowing world how these things came about." He promises to tell of "carnal, bloody and unnatural acts, of accidental judgments, casual slaughters, of deaths put on by cunning and forced cause, and in this upshot, purposes mistook, fallen on the inventor's head." "All this" Horatio pledges, he can "truly deliver."

But not waiting for this truest account, Fortinbras "summons the noblest," probably that his own election may proceed. While averring that he speaks sadly, he briskly embraces his fortune, claiming "rights of memory" that allow him to use his advantageous position. Horatio accedes to this, promising to speak on behalf of Hamlet in support of this claim, but recognizing that the practical must take precedence over a paraphrase of the past.

Fortinbras has the last word, giving Hamlet pyrrhic rites befitting a warrior: "for he was likely, had he been put on, to have proved most royally." While this saves Hamlet's "wounded name" and gives him an honored place in so-called "monumental history," surely a critical historian would prefer a fuller account of the facts and the values guiding them? Hamlet strove to prove his legitimacy and this is given him by Fortinbras. But haven't we seen why truth, even illegitimate or ugly, must be chosen over pious lies that bind souls to fury, betray the common good and pave a path to perdition? Should not each reader of *Hamlet* be his own Horatio? Can we expel the furies and turn a purged "hamlet" into a sanctuary for the better angels of our nature?

All I have done is show how a plausible case can be made for a reading of *Hamlet* that explains several unexplained issues in the play and is thoroughly consistent with Shakespeare's humane and erotic Christianity.

CHAPTER TWO
BREAKING FROM EUROPE:
A BASTARD, A BAD KING, AND THE BIRTH OF
BRITAIN IN *KING JOHN*

How did Shakespeare understand "England's Worst King" and what lessons should we derive from his portrayal of John? It is clear that the Bard has picked and chosen here; many relevant details, whether historical or not, are added to and excluded from the historical facts in a way suited to the lesson he teaches and the way he wishes to impart it. I will argue that he makes these changes as part of his endless exploration of human nature and the cosmic order that sustains it. It also seems that he provides us with many odd characters who serve as his spokespersons; these are often marginal eccentrics: the clowns, fools, and victims left in the wind and rain while Fortuna's favorites go back across the river to their warm palaces. Yet these losers, the ragged nobodies who went with Lear on his last journey, are those who must be interrogated about the final questions and contingent conclusions the Bard left as his corpus. Never forgetting John was a loser himself, we must follow this eccentric history closely and look for its poetic truth.

King John is either reviled or neglected by literary critics; reactionary or neo-conservative theorists cannot make it fit their Procrustean categories. They would prefer to "sit around and tell sad stories of the death of kings," whilst being oblivious to the play's intent. Like Homer's Agamemnon and Zeus, king and pope are selfishly blind to what's truly good; *King John's* unlikely hero, the Bastard, fights for his land or nation (not God), retaining his virtue while helping to heal an exploited people. He is proto-Protestant in that Protestantism restores the people as the true church or *ekklesia* and rejects priestly hegemony without denying the divine; in Classical terms, it gives us godly *Moly* or "love in idleness"—a power to behold a "thou" without a blinding Midas-lust for an objectified "it."

But even before reading *King John,* and meeting its bastard hero, we must resolve another question of legitimacy. Just as there are two intertwined realms, England and France, in Angevin times, there are also two plays: *The Troublesome Reign of King John* and *King John.* Which one of the two is the original or firstborn and which is the illegitimate copy or imitation? But this riddle only opens up a far more important question: What is legitimacy? Is the Church, king, or law the ultimate authority about what is just, good and true? Or is the true law written in our hearts? In so far as we know Shakespeare to have written *King John,* the better play, is this issue of legitimacy resolved and made moot despite our original question about origins and antecedents not having been answered? Is the matter best resolved through the gift of the logos: speaking together? This, after all, is the original meaning of the French word "parliament."

This play's author is no lover of papacy or political theology. Some claim that *King John* is less anti-Catholic than *The Troublesome Reign of King John* due to Shakespeare's supposed Catholic sympathies, but that may not be true. *King John* goes past the anti-papalism of *The Troublesome Reign of King John,* and even past historical Protestantism and the Roman Empire that executed Jesus, by resurrecting and revealing the true origins of Western Civilization: Greek Humanism. It also points us towards what Luther tried to suppress when the peasants revolted: the true import of Jesus' evangelical gospel or good news. *King John* indirectly defends the Renaissance and Reformation by exposing the ugly intrigue leading to England's first break with Rome. It holds an ironic attitude towards claims towards royal absolutism and divine right by exposing the viciously cynical and deeply flawed logic behind attempts to legitimize monarchic rule by appeal to divine or papal authority. Yet, in doing all this, *King John* steadfastly defends justice and the nation state, giving us a better and broader basis for regarding the common good.

Shakespeare's open-ended plays provoke us to contemplate and discuss them; his maieutic dramaturgy offers a fresh alternative to the old Church's stultifying dogma, the Puritans' incendiary fundamentalism, and Hobbes' Draconian synthesis of the two. Only the Bastard gains self-knowledge; he accepts both mother-soil and soiled mother. Indeed, he cannot really know his true father, given that his widowed mother has found a new riding-partner. But given her dead spouse's limitations, the Bastard's mother only resembles Queen Eleanor, who divorced Louis VII lamenting that she had married a priest. We also recall that since Kings Philip and John are both children of second marriages entered into while their father's first spouse was alive, they are both bastards—scripturally speaking—with the Church serving as pander to the adulterous coupling. Lastly, we even find that all the Norman-Angevin nobility featured in *King John* are also without mother soil, and thus worse than bastards, as they do not belong to either England or France. In the end, only the Bastard is seen to have true honor; he repudiates his undeserved property rights for a knighthood. Only he can speak for England. If his motherland is to be true to herself, as he urges, men such as he must be trusted to defend her sullied honor. Yet, if this does not suggest that all or most property is theft, although it surely was in Norman—Angevin England, does it at least mean that most propertied men are owned and only known by their secondary attributes or qualities and are thus willy-nilly alienated and estranged from their own true substance?

This idea is not necessarily Marxist. Even democracy is but the raw power of the mob or demos; without a proper conserving form it is just gift-wrapped for tyranny. The Bastard is an exceptional commoner who, like the Bard, speaks for the common good. In showing the evils of hereditary rule, *King John* delicately points us back to the old Saxon model of elected kingship; and past his time, towards parliamentary rule. The Bastard does not represent his dead ancestors, as peers do; he speaks for his times and people: He is a parliamentarian. This re-introduction of speech or *logos* mitigates the worst effects of Bastard William's conquest, made sacred by papal approval and force of arms.

Although Christianity is supposedly based on the revelation of Jesus as the Logos of God, this claim was blunted by a reactionary tradition starting after the fall of the Greek logos-based polis. Even if Aristotle had once defined man as political animal, he effectively denies logos as a political principle and suggests that men be ruled as animals by habit and mimesis. Worse yet, papal clericalism subverts its Christian origin in seeing man via Augustinian eyes as a fallen soul that cannot know or rule itself; thus, human rational speech, friendship and politics are denounced as sinful; instead man must be ruled for his own good by kings and popes. The popes demand total power over men by saying that they succeed Peter. They use Jesus' words to Peter in Matthew 16.19, "whatever you will bind on earth will be bound in heaven and whatever will be loosed on earth will be loosed in heaven," to claim absolute authority over mankind. To this was added the forged Donation of Constantine in which the Emperor was said to have ceded the West to Rome's bishop. Jesus' radically emancipatory gospel was betrayed earlier by Paul in Romans 13 when he said that all power came from God and required obedience to earthly authority. This submission became tradition and then holy law. This union of Petrine power and Pauline pusillanimity plagued Europe through the Middle Ages.

How are we to replace outrageous and illicit claims to authority from God via Peter and Paul to popes and kings? And how may we be good when the vertical logic linking man to God is fatally compromised? Even Nietzsche's Zarathustran imperative of fidelity to the Earth seems to involve making cunning and violent love to *Fortuna* and practicing Machiavellian virtue towards the fickle and irrational human material he plays the "Great Game" with. Can we speak of a good life or seek to live in a just community when (almost) all is ruled by vile necessity and only family is (said to be) sacred? *King John* pits a voluntary bastard against a vicious pope who calls himself Innocent and claims infallibility. But what if only a bastard can ask truly legitimate political questions *qua* outlaw? Only he may be the free spirit Nietzsche hoped for, a hero who could help overcome the absurd choice between a silent stagnant stability based on freshly forged dogma, and a horrid nihilistic chaos where all speech is rhetoric and everything is commodity. I will claim that *King John* reveals Shakespeare's loyalty to the Renaissance, the Reformation and the still unrealized humanistic dream of secular states bridging the gap between nature and nihilism. By its punning love of logos and language, *King John* gives us richly suggestive images that make discussion of the commonweal open to all of good will. If its spirit is not democratic, *King John's* turn from a self-serving nobility to a patriotic middle class is critical.

After the Bard's *alter-ego* Bottom has entered our world via mythic space in *A Midsummer Night's Dream*, he now enters historical time as the Bastard in *The Life and Death of King John*. If Shakespeare is trying to deny the belief in original sin and defy the dogma and deference accompanying this pernicious doctrine, which rejects all that the Renaissance and Christian Humanism stand for, it is fitting that a bastard, neither martyred Christ-figure nor self-nominated scourge of heaven, is the focus of the Bard's only

24

solely-written stand-alone English history play. And if Jesus, though not the son of his mother's husband, could bring redemption, perhaps the Bard's Bastard can give us something too?

The Bastard's role in *King John* is also redemptive. Even if the Bastard of Cognac barely exists in history, he stands for the potential in everyman. Said to be the son of Richard, the dead Achilles of *King John,* his birth is as unnatural as Bottom's liaison with Titania, and as lusty as David's liaison with Bathsheba. Once named Philip, he becomes the friend John sought in King Philip. Seeing Richard's killer "Austria" wearing his lionskin, like Hector in Achilles' armor, the Bastard slays him, hoping to do his father's business and even being England's warlord-messiah for a while. And just as he renounces his lands to be truly himself, so too must French land revert to France so England may be itself.

Much of the significance of *King John*'s opening scene would not have been lost on its 1590's English audience. A country only recently threatened with foreign invasion and understandably paranoid about papal subversion would respond with spirit to anyone speaking of the English king's "borrowed majesty." But the more discerning would also have known that English was not the language spoken in King John's court, even though he was the first King of England since the conquest who was born and buried there. It is also worth noting that Richard, his celebrated older brother, did not speak English at all, only French and Occitan. Indeed, it was only after the reign of Richard II (1377–1399) that English replaced French as the mother-tongue of the king of England. As we may recall, Shakespeare's Richard of Bordeaux viewed the populist familiarities Henry Bolingbroke showed towards the common people in a very dim light; speaking English was almost certainly one of them. This all serves to make the point that while any reference in *King John* to an Anglo-French divide would have appealed to deep-rooted prejudices in an Elizabethan theatre audience, such a response would have been strange to John or his courtiers; they would not have seen themselves as English.

Yet, after the French ambassador has been sent back with a message of defiance it is suggested that John's claim to the throne of England has as much to do with possession as right; while Angevin law prefers the child of an older son over a younger son, the Norman laws of succession favor the claims of any son over a grandson. In the final analysis it was as much through the support of Queen Eleanor and most of the English nobility as by the law that John prevailed. The main argument was pragmatic: John seemed better suited to rule England than the boy Arthur; as Shakespeare's audience would have known, a different approach was taken in Richard II's case. This would have led them to view John's case with greater sympathy, even if Philip of France had not intervened to back Arthur. By the end of *King John* we learn to avoid being seduced into seeing this play through the bloodshot eyes of a self-appointed scourge of heaven. Instead, we learn how to scrutinize a designated scapegoat with sympathy and understanding. At first, we take the easy way and champion Christlike Arthur against evil John. But he may not be the true scapegoat.

But first, the overall effect of this perplexing way *King John* poses the problem of the succession must be considered. The Bastard put it best when he said: "I am amazed, methinks and lose my way among the thorns and dangers of this world." Even if we ignore the moment of the Bastard's case, it must be evident that sacred laws of primogeniture are as abstract as Richard II's famous words about his holy status as an anointed king. The presence of prudential factors cannot be denied. And this brings into focus many troublesome matters that most would have preferred to ignore. Indeed, the very institution of the monarchy becomes the subject of profane human thought. It is small wonder that, when *Richard II* was revived during the Essex rebellion, Elizabeth saw herself as Richard of Bordeaux, reportedly saying, "I am Richard II, know ye not?" As soon as the sacred aura surrounding a monarch begins to dissipate, he or she becomes little better than a tightrope walker well aware that the price of failure is death. Is all majesty borrowed?

The implications of this question extend far beyond technical conflicts between Norman and Angevin legal systems; in the approximately sixty years before the staging of *King John,* England had gone through four revolutionary changes in religious practice and seen no fewer than four queens executed for treason. The parallels between the times of John and Elizabeth were far too obvious to need explication. Both monarchs had been regarded with suspicion by their immediate predecessor and were under excommunication from the Church; Rome would have rejoiced at news of their overthrow; also, for the first time in many centuries, both ruled over kingdoms without contiguous Continental possessions and under imminent threat of invasion. This is why neither ruler could take their "majesty" for granted; Elizabeth had recently executed her main rival, Mary, Queen of Scots, and John was about to openly call for Prince Arthur's death. Both victims could make plausible claim to the throne of England and both had the pope's support.

Given this context, we can see why our Bard could hardly give open expression to his own views on the, literally burning, religious or political matters *King John* deals with; perhaps it was safer for Shakespeare to seem to revise *The Troublesome Reign of King John*, an already popular anti-Catholic play, about a past era as many centuries removed from his time, as his is from our own. But even if *King John* precedes *The Troublesome Reign of King John*, and the latter is merely an illicit or bastard imitation of the original, *King John*'s Bastard is his own man. Existing through his shamelessly honest observations about the world he's thrown into, the Bastard owns himself and trusts in his own eyes and mother-wit as surely as he lacks both the material substance he gave away and is without factual proof of ever having lived. It follows that the Bard both is and is not responsible for all his Bastard says. To quote Duke Senior's remark about Touchstone in *As You Like It*: "He uses his folly like a stalking-horse, and under the presentation of that he shoots his wit." This illegitimate hero and reputed son of *Coeur de Lion* takes leave without leaving outward sign he ever existed. Yet he gives to England the heart King Richard reputedly tore out of a lion. The proof of this is that his country will never be invaded again.

The Bastard and his half-brother appear just after the French Ambassador has been sent off by King John; following dramatic precedent they depict in comic form what could not be explicitly discussed on stage, in a play that takes the form of a tragedy. Their dispute has to do with a dead man's estate; should the law or his will, supported by the self-evident truth, determine who inherits it? Although John feels that law, which gives the estate to the firstborn son in wedlock of the dead man's wife, should override the truth, once the Bastard discovers that he is the son of Richard, he is persuaded by Eleanor to renounce his legal rights and follow her to France. He thus emulates his father's heroic qualities, but also shows how they should be dedicated to his kingdom and are to be reincarnated in the gentlemen of England, not in the corrupt Angevin nobility; in short, neither Arthur nor John has inherited the mantle of idealized King Richard

Coeur de Lion. Also, France and Jerusalem are not the proper venues for the display of English virtue. This is symbolized in Richard's adulterous affair with the Bastard's mother; a parallel is drawn with King David's adultery with Bathsheba and his victimizing of Uriah the Hittite. The country will soon have to pay a heavy price for Richard's neglect of his primary obligation as king to serve England and its people. This too was a form of adultery. We see Shakespeare discuss this topic more explicitly in another tragedy written at almost the same time: *Richard II*.

The Bastard as he is portrayed in *King John* is significantly different from his counterpart in *The Troublesome Reign of King John*; Shakespeare's character is more than a brave young man who does not know his father's true identity. He is more Everyman than the Missing Prince of a romance tale. The Bastard in *King John* is also a sardonic observer of all that takes place before him. While he is preparing to replace Arthur as Eleanor's favorite grandson, his dry wit never deserts him. The Bastard makes some acute remarks that strike to the root of the absurd rules governing court manners that are strongly reminiscent of Touchstone and Jacques in another contemporary play: *As You Like It*. While Jacques sought to withdraw from the world while yet taking delight in his ability to "suck melancholy out of a song as a weasel sucks eggs," the Bastard recognizes that he must move with the current of the times. But he also plans, more ambiguously, "to deliver / Sweet, sweet, sweet poison for the age's tooth." While he hopes to employ this art not to "practice to deceive" but "to avoid deceit," he yet speaks of the age's "mounting spirit," and of using this same art to "strew the footsteps of my rising." He will not be the first would-be Machiavellian to be left drained and disgusted by his attempts to dominate Fortuna.

When joined by his mother, who finally confesses to her sin, the Bastard confidently shrives her, finding it no sin to be unable to resist the wooing of one who could take the heart of a lion. He is at least as grateful for not being the son of scrawny Sir Robert, "Madam I would not wish a better father," as Solomon presumably was for not being the son of Uriah the Hittite. Indeed, since Sir Robert was knighted instead of being sent to his death, the outcome seems to have been good for all parties involved. Neither his mother nor he can resist the "mounting spirit" of their age. It seems that nothing is fixed in its place by God and nature; the human soul is not a mighty fortress or fortified town, made capable by a combination of guilt and grace of denying itself any emotion not ordered by God and his pope.

The play resumes in Angers, the significantly named capital of John's French empire. Queen Eleanor's province of Aquitaine is ignored in *King John*; it is as if the four French provinces demanded of John in 1.i make up the entirety of his holdings in France; Brittany, already held by Arthur and inherited through Constance's father, was never John's to dispose of. Angers is being besieged by Philip of France, his former ally and friend. It was well known that King Philip urged John to rebel and claim the crown for himself when Richard was being held captive in Germany; in effect, John was led astray by Philip just as Richard was seducing the Bastard's mother while her benighted husband was sent abroad in his service. It would have been well known to *King John*'s audience that Philip's principal purpose was to break up the Angevin empire and make France great again; he also sought revenge for Eleanor's abandonment, humiliation and divorcing of his father: Louis VII. This is why he allied with all four sons of Henry II. But there may not be a real friendship here; Philip only sought to play the brothers off against each other and make common cause against their father. Now he repeats this practice with Arthur. While the wily king of the French has no claim to these provinces in his own right, by detaching them from John's virtual empire, he will be one step away from making them fully French. Indeed, it is to his advantage that Arthur only become ruler of these lands and Brittany, and not of all England as well—as he originally demanded of John; it would then be all that much easier for him to regain them. Even if Arthur did not lose Brittany and the Angevin lands right then, Philip would still be his king.

We also find out much more about Shakespeare's King John based on how he acts in Anger(s), for it is here that he comes to life. If *King John* is about the true Birth of Britain, we must surely study the character and conduct of the midwife who brought this state into being. Intentionally or not, by cutting the umbilical cords binding Angevin England to Continent and Church, permanently in one case and temporarily in the other, John brought about much weeping and gnashing of teeth. In spite of this, though, it seems as if sweet use was somehow made at the time by bastardized Britain from this adversity. Today, after another Brexit, eight hundred years after King John and over four centuries after Shakespeare's play about him, we could yet try to see how the wisest Englishman of them all beheld the relation of England to Europe in general and the prime mover behind the first split in particular. Even if the Bastard is the true hero of *King John* and if John, as implied, is just his midwife (John the Baptist), it is against the ugly backdrop of his king's waning that the Bastard reaches self-awareness as the soon to be personified spirit of Britain.

The French are already in position at Angers and, before the forces of John arrive, we come to see that King Philip is quite cynically using Arthur to advance his own interests. This is the first example of "commodity" that is brought to our attention. Even if Philip's ends are hardly evil, as we noted earlier, his histrionic posturing would not appeal to a spirited Elizabethan audience. But it sets them up for the rueful recognition that King John will soon be seen to be acting in an identical manner. This sense of symmetry is reinforced when Eleanor and Constance, mother-in-law and daughter-in-law, get into a screaming match, each accusing the other of unchaste behavior that would discredit the legitimacy, and claims to rule, of their respective sons. It also seems that their conflicting egos cloud any powers of objectivity they possess; this is of importance since the two angry mothers control the wills of their sons: John and Arthur. This parallel has the effect of infantilizing John. It also helps us to see that England must also strive for its own emancipation from France, the unreasonably demanding mother country. It must follow the Bastard's example.

The final example of this absurd symmetry is seen when the Bastard and "The Duke of Austria"—an equally fictional character compounded of two of Richard's enemies—also start insulting each other. It began when Austria first tried to silence the women and the Bastard supported him, only to be enraged when Austria, with ample reason, asks who he is; the Bastard now takes offense at a lion skin worn by Austria, apparently taken as a trophy from *Coeur de Lion's* corpse by his reputed killer. Acting as Richard's loyal son, the Bastard must see this as an insult. It is unclear if he is serious or not. As he warned us earlier, his "mounting spirit" will seek to "observe" and imitate the ways, "exterior form and outward accoutrement," of the "worshipful society" he is now in; it is evident that both senses of "observe" apply. The Bastard is both a critical watcher of, and mimetic participant in, the mad war-dance unfolding before him; *qua* actor, he is as ruled by his role as John, Philip, Eleanor and Constance are ruled by theirs. It is not only that *King John* imitates *The Troublesome Reign of King John*: there is also the sudden recognition gained by viewers of tragedy that the great must not be envied in their folly.

Caught up in the contagious calculus of commodity, the child Arthur and the city of Angers become costly counters in a cruel contest between clashing crowns. Though Arthur weeps and cries for peace, telling Constance, "I would that I were low laid in my grave, I am not worth this coil that's made for me," his words go unheeded. Once sprung, this cruel coil constructed completely from contingent chance cannot be casually collapsed and cast away. When the men of Angers also prove incapable of judging between opponents that match each other in bellicose bluster, claiming only to be "the King of England's subjects" but demanding proof of this identity before they admit their king, the question of Act I is now posed again: How is legitimacy demonstrated? If it could be passed about like a lion skin, that is at least sufficient proof for the day; but when it is held to be a transcendent quality, how on earth is it seen?

To put the question with extreme bluntness, if French-speaking Arthur has a better claim to the British crown than John, as his older brother's posthumous son, should not the English-born and English-speaking Bastard, accepted by Richard's mother and brother as the last king's only son, own a stronger right than either John or Arthur? Neither son knew his father. Why should an ink stained sheepskin command more respect than a lion skin? And worse, how can such a sheepskin allow one man rule the lives of a people or order those in an army to die for him? We note that marriage only became a sacrament of the Church in 1184, in John's lifetime, after the Council of Verona. Even more tellingly, the Archbishop of York in Richard's time and most of John's was Henry II's acknowledged son: Geoffrey.

There are three ways of resolving this question of legitimacy: convention, outright war and the wisdom of Solomon. The first is proposed by Hubert, a citizen of Angers, after bloody armed clashes produce no result other than the Bastard's idea (made in *The Troublesome Reign of King John* and *King John*) that the English and French forces first unite to take Angers, as the warring Jewish factions of doomed Jerusalem did when they were besieged Roman legions, before then letting Fortune decide. This idea is agreeable to both sides, as Angers is not their main prize; English forces will attack from the West while Austria and France assail the city from

North and South. The East is ignored. This plan pleases the Bastard even more; he hopes that French and Austrian guns will "shoot in each other's mouth," But Hubert proposes a marriage between Lewis and Blanche, John's niece. The union will not only save Angers but can also reconcile John and Philip, Richard's former friends, to each other. He warns that Angers' gates will never open if this solution does not win their favor.

The third possible solution is not explicitly stated but left implied by the reference to Jerusalem and the two angry whores fighting over the same child: Arthur. The wisdom of Solomon would consist in threatening to cut the baby up and letting the mother who loves the child more identify herself by giving it up. Just as the Biblical meaning had to do with the separation of the Kingdom of David and Solomon into Israel and Judah, here we see England and France fighting over the Kingdom of Henry II; the wisdom of Solomon would surely consist in deciding what's best for England and subtly ceding what's French to France. King John tries to do this. Seeming to heed Queen Eleanor's urgent advice that he save his crown, and preempt any chance that Arthur's (and hated Constance's) fortunes will exceed his, but without specific instructions or haggling, John yields to the Dauphin Lewis, and France itself, all his Norman and Angevin provinces and the huge sum of thirty thousand marks as his obscure niece Blanche's dowry.

Much of *King John*, II.1, is true only in a pedagogic-poetic sense rather than being historically accurate; Blanche was married to the Dauphin in 1200, long before John lost Anjou, Touraine, Maine and Brittany to King Philip. Then teenaged Arthur, offended by Philip's neglect of his interests in Blanche's marriage settlement, which did recognize English control over Brittany, first sought John's protection before fleeing back to France and revolting against England. If *King John*'s title character is neither Protestant hero, nor sadistic scapegoat in a Disneyesque morality play, how is he to be played? In exaggerating the seeming folly of John's readiness to gift lands he did not truly give up without a fight, the Shakespeare of *King John* may be hinting at something else. Contemporary tales of John, mainly penned by monks, show him in a darker light. But it is only late in Shakespeare's play that John, being placed in an untenable position by an evil cardinal and pope, succumbs to evil.

War is dangerous, expensive and unpredictable. It is attractive *tout court* only to prophets, psychopaths, profiteers and parasites. In making an offer the French cannot refuse, John may believe that he has chosen the path of peace with honor; no more playing Richard! But he and the other nobles may also be moved by cynical concerns. The public idiom of their peace-making, and the candied love talk of Eleanor and Lewis, reek of pandering. Even if the Bastard's apt tongue is ready to mouth and mock the court's cant, his nose is ill-prepared for its stench. So, haunted Hamlet-like by Richard, his absent father, the Bastard must grapple with lies far below the courtly games he seeks to play. This is why we must study his dazed response to the peace; he has lost a chance to be Richard. His glorious father also died besieging a castle for treasure; are the gutsy Bastard's truest motives also greed and glory? In short, Eleanor saw signs of Richard, her favorite son, in him. This made the Bastard disinherit himself, leave England, follow her to France. But he now sees John disinherit himself of a burden he could not hold. What does time hold for them?

The Bastard's response to Hubert's defiant words urging peace and threatening resistance suggest that they struck somewhere deep within his psyche. He himself had casually spoken of levelling Angers and then fighting France in language just as inauthentic as that used by the courtiers around him. It was he himself who spoke "as familiarly of roaring lions, as maids of thirteen do of puppy dogs." It was in this silly humor that he sought to imitate *Coeur de Lion*. This is why, admitting that Hubert "speaks plain cannon," the Bastard concedes that he "buffets better than the fist of France." His words are wary but they esoterically grant that receiving a scolding from Angers is better than being thrown into the scalding cauldron of a French war. A personal reference makes his meaning clearer: "Zounds, I was never so bethumped with words since I first called my brother's father Dad." There is a vast abyss between idle words and their true import in psychic or existential reality; despite his readily ridiculed looks, or perhaps due to them, Sir Robert would not have taken kindly to being called Dad by a living reminder of his wife's infidelity; it is this anger, not any highfalutin idea of aristocratic honor, that levels pride and makes all men equal to each other.

Though he once went at the ladder of honor and hierarchy with an eager "mounting spirit," seeking France to fight for Fortuna beside Queen Eleanor of the troubadours, the Bastard is now aware that he has fallen and landed in some squat abyss, a crass context characterized by cutthroat competition, calculated cruelty, and constant creative chaos. This is the unflattering but flattened terrain where the Bastard finds himself. Here, where the lowest common denominator is the Hobbesian fear of death, the highest value, worshipped by kings, is commodity. It has apparently led John, in order "to stop Arthur's title in the whole," to give up a large part of his Angevin empire. The Bastard is sure that the king chooses "willingly" to do so, not from love for peace or niece, but out of fear and the shameless wish for a comfortable life. It must also be borne in mind that the alternative to vulgar commodity is endless insatiable two-faced war. Shakespeare is clearly familiar with the essence of the argument Hobbes will make for a craven commodious life fifty years later.

The complete range of meaning covered by the catchphrase *commodity* covers such concepts as utility, comfort and convenience. Commodities are objects, matter in motion, that circulate to create a crass but ceaseless economy that replaces the cosmic spheres and changeless order of nature contemplated by Aristotle, Aquinas and Creation's God. This means that the ancient distinction between the Hyper-Uranian and the Sublunary, the eternal and the malleable, is no longer valid. Everything is matter in motion and further, to be very clear, only things or objects have existence. There are outlaw objects outside the economy of commodity but within it is violently imposed order and hypocrisy.

This law of commodity works the most ironic miracles in the serviceable lovers, leading Lewis to say, "I do protest I never loved myself, till now...I beheld myself, drawn in the flattering table of her eye." Blanche unblushingly responds that, whatever her uncle loves, "I can with ease, translate it to my will...and enforce it easily to my love." In response, the Bastard reflects, "This is pity now ... there should be in such a love, so vile a lout as he." Whether or not, out of love or vaulting ambition, he wanted Blanche for himself, he can only cry, "Mad world, mad kings, mad composition." This craven spirit of commodity is surely as injurious to the human spirit as war is to our poor bodies.

The Bastard's famous speech on commodity is now uttered in disgust as he finds that the metaphysical principle that mesmerizes modernity is commodity. Although a Cardinal will soon appear, claiming to be exempt from its totalizing force, we soon find that he is but the missing cardinal point in the compass of European influence that was drawn earlier, with the three main kingdoms of France, England and Austria having points in the South, West and North respectively. The compass is fully boxed once we accept the pope's temporal presence at the Eastern march or limits of European Christendom. This is Europe's First Commodious Market. Whether or not he can successfully manage a Brexit or Exodus from this insidiously looming leviathan, the Bastard's passionately prophetic account of its essential features is worth our attention, even today.

The Bastard talks of commodity as one not immune to its charms: He is a wise virgin by virtue of not being worth corrupting. He has "rich eyes and empty hands"; this is how he sees that commodity is a "purpose-changer," "break-vow" and "bias of the world (otherwise) well made to run even on even ground." Thus, "smooth-faced" commodity is like a snake that seduces the direction of a community away from fulfilling their common good and toward the selfish "gaming" of reality. By this open hostility to community, and the common good, commodity turns its duped victims into objects who see themselves as sovereign rulers and masters of reality. Admitting that he only rails on this power "because he has not wooed me yet," the Bastard ends his tirade by praying to commodity, shamelessly calling it by its true name: "Since kings break faith upon commodity, Gain be my lord, for I will worship thee!"

Sincerely or not, the Bastard, while trying to live by the day's ruling spirit, now gripes that Philip, "fickle France," is led by commodity, "this bawd, this broker," "from his own determined aid, from a resolved and honorable war, to a most base and most vile-concluded peace." The equivocal words reflect a divided soul. His prayer to Commodity is countered or matched by Constance's furious response to the news of the peace and impending marriage. Crying out "war, war," and effortlessly moving between the roles of war-mongering fury and *mater dolorosa*, she curses France and "strumpet Fortune" for betraying her perfect, beautiful boy while rejecting his comfort. Both Constance and the Bastard are children of the Age of Commodity, seeking war and profit over peace and virtue. While Constance must feel in her heart that she played the game and lost, the Bastard yet tries to play on for goods he knows to be empty.

Their several prayers and curses are answered just after the ceremony marrying Lewis and Blanche has ended; there is reality beyond the ordered realm of commodity. Even as King Philip proclaims an annual holiday to mark this "blessed day," he is angrily interrupted by a furious Constance. She curses the day, saying, "You came in arms to spill mine enemies' blood, but now in arms you strengthen it with yours," repeatedly asking "the heavens" to "set armed discord 'twixt these perjured Kings." She has no shame about seeking strife for private reasons; even the Bastard never yearned for war as she does. We now see why Queen Eleanor fears and dislikes her so much. As self-righteous as Juno and bitter as Dido, Constance uses vivid Old Testament imagery to liken Arthur and herself to Jesus and Mary menaced by Herod-like John. Philip, having washed his hands of them, is another Pontius Pilate.

Constance now turns on Austria, calling him a slave and coward; mocking the lionskin he wears as Richard's killer, she suggests he "hang a calf's skin on those recreant limbs" instead. When he bristles at her words, "O that a man should speak these words to me," the Bastard gleefully repeats them—spoiling for a fight and anxious to prove his legitimate ownership of the lionskin. But even as John, leaving the plot of *The Troublesome Reign of King John,* struggles to silence him ("thou dost forget thyself"), a papal legate arrives as a *deus ex machina,* in seeming response to Constance's powerful curses.

The inference may be drawn that this papal intervention from the East is not ruled by the selfish laws of commodity governing England, France and Austria. This pope zealously asserted his presumed powers as successor to St. Peter by unilaterally and arbitrarily naming his old friend from the Sorbonne, Stephen Langton, Archbishop of Canterbury, the Primate of All England, over John's head. Innocent III, in *King John* and also in historical fact, embodies the false and foolish papal absolutism inaugurated by Gregory VII a generation earlier. Holy Mother Church, outranking both Eleanor and Constance, claims maternal authority over John and Philip in ways that violate the integrity of both kings and their countries. Even if John is on shaky ground in proclaiming supremacy over the English Church, he is quite correct to find it absurd that an Italian priest, a cardinal-nephew, elected by twenty-one Italian clerics (of whom five were cardinal-nephews—papal relatives chosen by him) should lay claim to ultimate power over all of Western Europe.

History shows that Innocent III's main concern was the absolute assertion of papal power; among other things, he was responsible for such atrocities as the Albigensian Crusade which slaughtered over 20,000 Christians in Southern France, the Fourth Crusade's sack of Christian Byzantium and the Fourth Lateran Council's bans on Jews holding public offices or appearing without a yellow star. This latter provision was ecumenically extended to Muslims also. It seems that the only alternative to commodity is arbitrary power, whether religious or not. Yet, as this ethic is also ruled by hidden self-interest, even if this is also hidden from oneself, it still comes under the category of commodity. Hobbes saw that there is no true or lasting happiness in a world of matter in motion ruled by selfishness; the only difference is that while commodious life is a war of all against all, theocracy's selfish guardians rule stupid slaves.

Following this model, the papacy's only real value is in serving as a sort of ontological backstop; it provides a world of bastards with gravity if not legitimacy. But it can only do so by serving as an unmoved mover. The moment the pope overtly enters the field of commodity, he unsettles all authority, his own included. As we shall soon observe, John and Innocent inflict grievous harm to each other's vital interests by violating this non-aggression pact. This is the hidden meaning behind the Bastard's/Shakespeare's gleeful repetition of the phrase, "hang a calf's skin on those recreant limbs." More elegant words will soon be used to argue against the need for John's second crowning but the import is the same: Protestants must not protest too much and neither should a Papal Bull be written on a calf's hide.

Returning to *King John,* we see John respond to the pope by refusing to accept Langton. Declaring himself "supreme head" of the Church "under God" in his dominions, John also refuses to send any more money to Rome. When Philip warns him against blasphemy, John will not back down. Calling Pandulph a "meddling priest," the words his father spoke of Beckett, he accuses the pope of "juggling witchcraft with revenue" for he "sells pardon from himself." Even if everyone else "cherishes" these abuses, John will "oppose against the Pope and count his friends my foes." It is noteworthy that while John does not use Henry II's words dooming Beckett in *The Troublesome Reign of King John,* he makes a more explicit claim there "to reign next to God, supreme head both over spiritual and temporal." The effect, subtle though it may be, is to focus more on Roman interference and abuses rather than to make grandiose claims about reigning next to God, with power equal to that supposedly granted Peter. This makes *King*

John's John at this point much more like Henry II or Elizabeth than Henry VIII. It is *Troublesome Reign*'s King John who threatens to make anyone contradicting "him hop headless."

The papal decree that John is "cursed and excommunicated" turns from talk of friends and foes to using God's name in vain to bless and curse. The pope deems "meritorious," "canonized and worshipped as a saint," any "hand" "that takes away by any secret course thy hateful life." This power of cursing is jealously guarded by the Church; this is made clear to angry Constance. On asking Pandulph, in his capacity as papal legate to "cry Amen" to her curses, she is brusquely told, "There's law and warrant, lady, for my curse." Her counter, "when law can do no right, let it be lawful that law bar no wrong," as good an argument for John's case against the pope and his Church, as hers is against him, is unanswered. This is partly since, in ironic sequence, and apt response to her words, Philip now takes John's hand.

In *King John*, as opposed to *The Troublesome Reign of King John*, King Philip is portrayed quite sympathetically. He seems to be genuinely conflicted over how best to proceed here. The first French ruler to call himself King of France, he was first Richard's friend against Henry II and then John's friend against Richard, but his first loyalty was always to France. In this, he is much unlike Richard: *Coeur de Lion* valued glory, the Crusades and French wars above England. While this endeared Richard to his barons, who sought always to keep their French landholdings, it did not serve the best interests of England or the English. Thus, by implied contrast to Richard, Philip is the role model for the nation building *King John* points toward. Yet John shows himself to be an even better steward to his land by standing up to the pope and risking excommunication.

But although Philip is well disposed towards John, who has offered him everything he really wanted for France, the sentence of excommunication changes everything. Philip runs the risk of excommunication himself. This, given the threadbare state of his nascent kingdom, would undo all its ruler has done. His unruly barons will tear France apart. While *King John* does not mention this, the hullabaloo of conflicting voices urging him to break from, or ally, with John (with Lewis, Constance and Austria backing the pope, while Blanche and Eleanor side with John) reflects this spirit. Even the Bastard's voice, obsessively following his feud with Austria, reflects similar qualities in Philip's soul. And Austria is not truly France's friend; they are but contingently joined in hostility to John. Austria may turn on France.

Ultimately Philip must disregard his soul's voice and do what commodity and realpolitik advocate. The pope has the bigger battalions on his side and will prevail. While Philip is far saner than either Brutus or Hamlet, the ugly inner strife he undergoes is just as intense and qualitatively similar: In all three cases a decent man's personal conscience and enlightened reason are opposed to irrational emotional suasion and all the pressure of tradition and convention. Needless to say, Innocent III's papacy stands for the latter side of this equation; while the Church and its threat of excommunication smother his conscience, Philip's rationality is overwhelmed by crassly commodious calculation.

The scales were first unbalanced by false commodities like honor and faith. As Lewis, more thumotic than his sire, values Rome's curse more than England's friendship, Constance begged of Philip that he value faith and his soul, both represented by Pandulph, above friendship with England. When Blanche contends that Constance's faith-based reasons come from her need (for revenge), Constance claims that all faith comes from need, all is commodity again. Philip now turns to Pandulph, arguing that breaking the peace breeds revenge and bloodshed, violating honor and tainting faith. He gives these values real content, placing them beside the equally virtuous act of averting bloody war.

Pandulph responds by adding a terrifying nihilistic element on Philip's scales; replying to the king's plea that he "impose some gentle order" in this fraught situation, the Cardinal pronounces: "All form is formless, order orderless, save what is opposite to England's love." Just as the breath of God brought life out of the primal chaos existing at the moment of the earth's creation, nothing on earth has any order or integrity outside the will of the pope. In fine, the Church has no friends, only temporary alliances with the enemies of its enemies. Government, as St. Augustine charitably reminds us, is not for the sake of the Good Life; it is humanity's punishment for Original Sin. And this, as we must know, came about through disobedience. France must obey her holy Mother, "Be champion of our church, or let the church our mother breathe her curse." England is compared to a serpent whom Philip holds by its tongue. Perfidious Albion cannot be trusted to keep her word; even if she did, trusting her and disobeying the church is a sin.

Still desperately seeking a way out, Philip drops John's hand saying, "I may disjoin my hand but not my faith." The equivocal words hint that while he will not dishonor the church by being friends with John, Philip will not break faith by betraying John. Faith could have two dimensions: Vertical faith is friendship with man and horizontal faith ties him to God. But Pandulph responds that all oaths derive their authority from the sacred coronation vow a king makes to heaven when he swears to be the champion of the church. This mother of all vows is made to holy mother church, said to be identical with God. So, despite Jesus' words asking us not to swear, but say only yes and no, a king is bound and linked by a chain of oaths to heaven that supersedes any other bond he enters into. This primal oath to heaven, and *a fortiori* to church and pope, binds or loosens all others; it is also a king's sacred honor and identity.

Pandulph means that by not fighting John, Philip ceases to be king; this makes both France and Lewis illegitimate. France and its king owe their power to sworn lines of legitimacy drawn from a dim past but guaranteed by the pope. These words may merely build vertical chains of pious fools, keepers of dead oaths made to piles of dust and bones in graveyards, as opposed to a horizontal pride of line-dancing lions, free spirits laughing at burden-bearing camels, but the choice is stark and clear. When the legate now threatens to curse Philip too, the king says, "There is no need. England I will fall from thee." Philip joins the holy fools, while John is left with the bastards, knaves and outlaws.

Philip's use of "fall" and "England" is striking. He admits implicitly that he is acting in "bad faith" and is reluctant to address England's king by name. John responds in kind, telling "France," "Thou shall rue this hour within this hour." Philip has tried to look at the next life while ignoring reality. John is "burned up with inflaming wrath," a rage only blood can allay. Philip replies, "Thy rage shall burn thee up ... look to thyself, thou art in jeopardy." Both men talk of Hell as if it is a psychic state on earth. They may not believe in an afterlife but feel the effects of a second fall. As noted before, Pandulph had his way by threatening the integrity of Philip and France. Since England and France are still too ill-defined to have firm identity, both rulers will be forced into war to keep legitimacy. As long as Philip got what he sought from John in Normandy and Anjou, France was a satiated power; but now with the treaty broken, angry John will fight for his empire, his barons desirous of keeping their French holdings even if John and Eleanor do not want war, and Constance will join Pandulph in urging Philip to fight for France, Arthur and the Church. We must also note that the Church prefers fluid frontiers; it does not like strong nation states that could check its power.

As Act III continues we see John, consumed with rage at this betrayal, seeking to make France feel his wrath as soon as possible. He ignores Philip's warning that his famed Plantagenet ire burns to his peril; even as Arthur is captured, Eleanor rescued, Austria killed, and the French are defeated, John now falls victim to his own demons. As Pandulph, whom John called a "meddling priest," shrewdly foresaw, John this time in indirect deed rather than word, rashly re-enacts the Beckett debacle. His folly is greater that his father's since Arthur, unlike Beckett, was held safely in his custody. Also, where Henry was justified in his rage at Beckett, who used clerical privilege to conceal his perfidious conduct, *King John*'s Arthur is an angelic child, quite unlike the rebellious and bratty teenager of *The Troublesome Reign of King John*. It seems that *King John* shows us the difference between clerically defined offenses against the church, and a genuine crime that pollutes its culprit's soul.

King John also implies a distinction between the Bastard's revenge killing of Austria and John's order to kill sinless Arthur. While the Bastard's deed is neither dastardly nor admirable but parallels Hamlet's desire to prove his legitimacy by retaliation, John may become illegitimate by an indirect act seeming to place him in the moral company of Herod. Hence it could also be the case that the Bard is testing us. Just as Richard III tempts us to side with a murderer, *King John* could be depicting an anti-heroic ruler, who has served England prudently but not pompously, being accused of pusillanimity.

The last scenes of Act III also draw a highly suggestive parallel between John, who ordered and intended the murder of Arthur, and Pandulph, who not only predicts and exploits Arthur's death but also cynically stoked a situation that increased its likelihood; if John and Philip had been reconciled, Arthur would not have been such a danger to John. As his readiness to give up land for peace shows, John is not like Richard; he does not enjoy war and killing as such. John's acts are ruled by the code of commodity; they do not come from a criminal character or crass concupiscence. So Pandulph is the wickeder of the two; his calculated acts come from outside the pale of commodity and necessity. Two kings are his puppets; one is ruled by fear of excommunication and the other lives in terror of being deposed.

John's order to kill Arthur in *King John* is given more deliberately than Henry II's hasty words about Beckett. After sending the Bastard off to pillage England's abbots (to fund a war stoked by the Church), and leaving Eleanor to speak with Arthur, John takes Hubert's hand. Following the symbolic economy of *King John,* it seems as if Hubert is replacing Philip as John's closest friend; we recall that he had earlier accepted Hubert's advice as to how the impasse over Angers could be resolved. Hubert's advice then made Arthur redundant. John now wants Hubert, who has just said that he was bound to John, to take the next step, but will not at first say so explicitly. Inviting Hubert to read his soul, in effect to be the body that does his will, and pointing Arthur out to Hubert and calling him "a very serpent" that is perpetually underfoot, John then assigns Hubert as Arthur's keeper. When Hubert pledges, "he shall not offend your majesty," John speaks tersely twice: "Death" and "a grave." Hubert's only responses are "My lord" and "he shall not live." At this, John cuts him short: "Enough. I could be merry now. Hubert, I love thee." After receiving Eleanor's blessing, for she has now silently rejoined them with Arthur, he leaves for Calais while Hubert and Arthur sail to England.

Is John's choice to order Arthur's death implicit, involuntary, hastily voluntary, or cold-bloodedly deliberate? How does it compare to Philip's betrayal of John? If Philip had bravely stuck by John and gained the Angevin lands as promised, he could have faced the threat of excommunication; his now unified people would probably have stood by France's first true king. When Philip warned John against anger, perhaps he should have looked to his own soul and known that the real harm caused by cowardice and betrayal exceeds the possible effects of excommunication; it is fair to say that his decision to abandon John was ultimately ruled by a blend of moral pusillanimity and commodity.

What then of John? Could he claim that Arthur had to die to stop civil war, for the sake of the realm? Is John more Caiaphas than Herod? While this could have been truer if said of *Troublesome Reign's* teenaged Arthur, the sacrifice of a life on the altar of commodity is still wrong. But could this have been said just after Mary of Scot's death? Much of the action in *King John* is in line with the ethic of expediency practiced on John's age, Shakespeare's, or ours. The big change, and the Bard deserves credit for this, is that we have learned to view ugly "acts of state" critically; also, if some dark deeds are justified in the name of necessity, they must not be shrouded in secrecy or made sacred in a way that turns killers into heroes. Souls only heal from violence when reasons are given and forgiveness is sought; if not, chains of sacred secrecy bind us to the past and drag us to Hell. They divide victims from knowers and doers in a way that harms all. *King John* shows how lusty youth, like the Bastard, can be shown life's horrors and eventually emerge better and stronger, while the alternative is to be exposed to a cynical logic of necessity that poisons the mind and tempts a soul to wither away. In the latter case, friendship and speech, the basis of true politics, become impossible as wounded souls shy away from self-knowledge. This state is well suited for theocratic persuasion, but the common good is badly served.

The Bard has Pandulph, the convener of the deadly Manichean chess game between England and France that only ended 250 years later, seem to explain his thinking to the French after John's initial success against them. He does this to encourage Philip to keep fighting John, and even charts a path that takes Lewis' "foot to England's throne." As with the Bush-Cheney invasion of Iraq, the thought was that this liberating force would be greeted with flowers. He does not tell Lewis that he fights as the pope's proxy, or that papal support will be withdrawn once John submits. Pandulph's prophecy is based on probability; it is as performative as the witches' predictions will be in *Macbeth*. Commodity's cockpit is ruled by a negative dialectic that pushes self-interest as much as it prevents self-knowledge. It is only in seeming madness, beyond its soul-killing collective sanity, that one sees the ugly truth about commodity.

The cold-blooded way Pandulph sees Arthur as a scapegoat tethered to tempt John is striking since Constance, his mother, has just left madly mourning her loss. Though the two are but separated and Arthur is not thought dead by anyone else, we realize that Pandulph's reason and Constance's grief both see the same tragic inevitability. Even as the Church forbids Constance suicide, it deliberately deploys Arthur like a pawn to take England; many fine young English Jesuits were sent home from Rome to be martyred in the same calculating spirit. The child must be offered up so that John will fall and Rome will triumph. And this image hides another, even more terrible parallel. Arthur, an innocent Jesus figure, is to be sacrificed for the greater glory of Pope Innocent and the Church. In keeping with the logic of commodity a fine statue or stained-glass window, featuring Constance and Arthur as a Madonna and Child, will surely be commissioned after his death. It will complement one of Beckett. As with Constance's one grey hair, it is better that one should be sacrificed for the image's artistic power. Each hair on her head is counted on. After this tragic display, she will be taken to Hamlet's nunnery and her guilty locks bound up. As she is told "Bind up those tresses" and "Bind up your hairs," crass commodity hisses *Bind up your heir* to angry suspicious John.

Pandulph's corrosive skepticism also extends to miracles. The cardinal cannot imagine a situation where compassion would make John or Hubert spare Arthur. Christian charity, which is managed by the Church, replaces natural compassion. Man can do good only by the grace of Christ who died for our sins. Selfish as we are, we only practice charity to reach Heaven. Pandulph preaches original sin and cold-bloodedly believes that all are ruled by evil necessity. Yet he also believes that artificial miracles and divine signs are necessary for belief in the Church to thrive. To this end, he will have his agents interpret any random event and natural aberration as a sign of God's anger at John. Most ironically, this "meddling priest" will depict John as Caiaphas while actually, or also, playing this very role himself.

The Bard seems to reveal his own belief in natural charity when he describes Arthur's interaction with Hubert. *The Troublesome Reign of King John* has Arthur persuade Hubert using explicitly Christian language; this suggests that Hubert is at least as much moved by fear of God as love of man. Yet since *King John* shows us that our friends can change hearts and influence actions, the inference follows that Pandulph's Church, Catholic in the sense of being concerned with all and of interfering in everything, is bad company for England. It is Holy only in the sense of being wholly concerned with its own power. Pandulph stands above commodity's chessboard while John is now sent beneath it. Both seem to see more clearly.

Hubert is named after St. Hubert, said to have been a son to an early Duke of Aquitaine and patron saint of humane hunters. He was converted while chasing a stag on Good Friday. His prey halted and, as a cross emerged between its antlers, the amazed huntsman heard a voice warning him that he risked going to hell unless he turned his life around. The stag told St. Hubert what Philip told John; but this Hubert hears his namesake's words better than his king's. In each case self-knowledge is urged; yet we must ponder if this way of being anti-commodious comes from the church or through friends. While John wished Hubert to embody his bad thoughts of Arthur, and Pandulph created a context where this malevolence was all but inevitable, Arthur preserves himself by just making Hubert look at his own soul; in effect, he turns into the hunted, cross-bearing, stag and his would-be killer Hubert becomes his sainted namesake.

While *The Troublesome Reign of King John's* teenaged Prince Arthur curses John, argues about law and tyranny, and threatens Hubert with hell-fire to save his life, his younger namesake in *King John* is more like the baby Jesus. Even as Hubert prepared the hot irons to burn out Arthur's eyes, his hardened custodian's eyes, blinded to compassion by extended direct exposure to commodious life, are given the gift of sight by the little prince. As noted this miraculous "event" is one of direct human vision; it is not mediated through commodity, the hope of future reward from Arthur, or by a religious appeal to show mercy in the name of Christ who died for our sins. The true human miracle is in Hubert's seeing Arthur for who he truly is: a harmless little boy who has been used by adults, all his life, to serve their own nefarious, fearful or ignorant ends. And Arthur, likewise, has treated Hubert with Christian love, ignoring his harsh appearance by some strange grace.

Far from cursing John, Arthur admits that his uncle and he fear each other, and goes on to lament his posthumous parentage. Even as Hubert tries to take refuge in the bad faith of being a slave sworn to duty (the same *chain of fools* image Philip succumbed to), and, in order to escape the guilt of pronouncing John's cruel sentence, makes Arthur read the order to blind him, his victim simply asks, "have you the heart?" After this pithy challenge, Hubert, who had successfully defended Angers against two royal armies, slowly gives in to the prince's persuasion. We may say that Arthur relieves Hubert of his blinded, misdirected, and fortified anger to give him self-knowledge. Even if this mad rage is revived ("you will but make it blush, and glow with shame at your proceedings, Hubert. Nay, perchance it will sparkle in your eyes, and like a dog that is compelled to fight, snatch at his master that doth tar it on"), Hubert will now feel shame or anger at himself. This is the proper office of the *thumos* that was misdirected outwards.

Spoken with the friendly simplicity of Jesus talking with the Elders at the temple steps, Arthur's words help Hubert see that evil only resides in the heart of man; in short it is we who commoditize, weaponize and kill nature, creating murderous necessities from harmless goods made for comfort. He prays that Hubert see the mote/moat (of tears?) in his own eye that checks him from seeing: "feeling what small things are boisterous there, your vile intent must needs seem horrible." Now seeing truly, Hubert says, "I will not touch thine eye for all the treasure thine uncle owns." Arthur replies, "you look like Hubert. All this while, you were disguised." Hubert then pledges, "Your uncle must not know but you are dead. I'll fill those dogged spies with false reports." But this only brings England to a rolling boil; false news and chains of fools soon overwhelm reality.

Arthur's loving words bite at Hubert's psychic chains the way Socrates' *daimon* disrupted the commodious vision of Athens. Only friends help us see life or our own souls rightly. And even if friendship is divine and not the friend, the divine speaks through friends. But as a friend is not a god, we cannot expect them to be godly all the time. At the very least this means that Arthur is not Jesus, Christ, or any sort of warlord-messiah. The implication is that Arthur cannot always be fearless and inspiring. He has no miraculous powers either. Indeed, like the mythic Arthur or even Jesus, he may only be himself posthumously; thus, the logos or conversation about, and practice of, a good life well lived matter more than exact identity with speaker or doer. Arthur and Socrates were both holy ignorant losers. This made them Jesus-like in a commodious world. But their foolish virtue helped them to live and die with integrity and without hate. It also means that they cannot easily leave their best qualities to us; as Antony said in *Julius Caesar*: "the evil men do lives after them, the good is oft interred with their bones." This is why Christian humanism is given and inherited in a way that makes us all ignorant bastards, fatherless and childless, with rich eyes and empty hands.

But since Arthur is too young and innocent to be a Christian king, for he and his mother will be tools of murderous Austria, whom he has too easily forgiven, and especially after pope and Pandulph have tarnished Christian values, how is England to be ruled? John's plight is worsened by having to succeed another impossible archetypal figure, *Coeur de Lion*. The anti-Christ-warlord-messiah died after bleeding England's coffers dry by his costly Crusade, endless French wars and huge ransom; it was as if he reprised his exploit with the lion by ripping all the gold from the land as John was said to pull teeth from Jews. Ill-suited to be Arthur or Richard, John must repair a ravaged realm when he returns to England. The rest of *King John* occurs here. England's kings will no longer be absentee landlords.

After the ahistorical sequence of events described in Acts I to III we can find many reasons to explain King John's second coronation. Though Arthur's removal leaves John with an unquestioned claim to the crown, this could hardly be heralded to England. But as his papal excommunication included a blessing for those who revolt against him, and even the promise of sainthood for his assassin, we see why a second crowning may have been used to proclaim John as the English Church's supreme head, answerable only to God. This will also be an apt occasion for the assembled English peers and clergy to pledge their loyalty to their king in his ongoing battle with the pope and French king. But the real struggle now is not for the Angevin estates in France; England itself is menaced by Philip and Innocent.

Yet following the event, which also reaffirms the king's ties to England, John's peers, who only enter the play at this point, already seem dissatisfied. While we can have no doubt that the Bastard has not only taken money from the rich abbots but also made similar demands on the barons and bishops, for while he is socially not one of them he is also just as ruthless as Richard, this may not be the only reason for their dissatisfaction. John cannot afford to forget that Philip and the pope have also been stirring up trouble for him at home. This would be very easy for them since, beyond the obvious ties the religious have with Rome, many of the greatest lords in the lands, who are mostly of Norman origin, have vast estates in France that may be in jeopardy. Neither party wants English independence; we may think of their relatives, in Shakespeare's age and in ours, who opposed Irish freedom from the same motive. But since it is hard to give open voice to these shameful and selfish concerns, or to admit to having been pressured by foreign powers, feigned concern for Arthur's welfare must serve as their watchword. The emergence of France as a nation state in the making has changed everything. It is now too expensive to be both English and French. Nor can we deny the pressure exerted by Innocent's power-hungry Church. England is torn apart in three different directions.

All this talk of gilding gold, painting lilies or perfuming violets suggests that John protests too much, that he risks destabilizing a loyal kingdom united behind him. But this is not simply the case; many barons and bishops could well be deeply embarrassed at having been made to swear allegiance to John while plotting against him. If anything, John's doubling down could be seen as denying the bivalent condition that had marked England since the Conquest or even before it. As such, Normans, Angevins or Romans cannot have a decisive voice in defining what is just or true to what is still a mostly Anglo-Saxon populace. These alien criteria must be found illegitimate. But even if their reasons for hating John are disingenuous, superficial and contrived, England's selfish aristocracy is yet a threat to the land. Salisbury embodies this hypocrisy. Despite his loudly professed aristocratic contempt for John, Hubert and their like, he is but a royal bastard hiding behind his earl's title. This basic dishonesty about who he is makes Salisbury a gilded bastard; he is easily gelded by his Francophone peers and duly becomes roped into their treasonous plots. Yet, as a native to the land, he should be able to read Hubert's true nature rightly.

There is also the matter of Hubert's "false reports," aimed at convincing John of Arthur's death. We soon find out that Hubert openly displayed a warrant for Arthur's death issued by John. It could be that Hubert received such an instrument, not as he obtained the one calling for Arthur's blinding, but only to blind John as to his true intention. But the more Hubert tries to protect Arthur in this way, the more he incriminates John and confirms the ugly rumors circulated from Paris and Rome. While *The Troublesome Reign of King John*'s Hubert tells John and his Lords that Arthur died after being blinded on John's instructions and the king rejoices, the false news of Arthur's death is secretly whispered to John by Hubert in *King John*. His well-meant misinformation has led to an ugly situation where both sides find that they prefer Arthur dead. As much as he seeks to avoid blame for it in *King John,* John now sees Arthur's value as a symbol of resistance to him; meanwhile the Barons planning to depose John see every advantage in finding the body and publicizing the death of Arthur, who had far better claim to be king than Lewis. This is why they speed off to find his corpse and display it.

While Hubert may sincerely believe that he is saving John from evil by sparing Arthur and circulating these rumors, they only increase John's paranoia and give his enemies further plausible cause to unite against him. In reality, they probably could not have cared about Arthur as a person, the people even less than the nobility. Geoffrey barely spent any time in England, and Arthur identified more with Brittany than Britain. But Arthur's death provided the perfect pretext for John's enemies to rally around Lewis, supposedly to be revenged on his killer, but really to rejoin France. They are outraged because of what he was, warlord messiah, rather than who Arthur, Hubert's friend, really was. This distinction applies to Jesus; the most ardent Christians are outraged at the killing of Christ but they do not heed the message of Jesus. Christ can be accommodated to their religion of commodity; Jesus, Mary's bastard son, cannot.

Meanwhile, bad news pours in from all sides. No sooner have the peers left after accusing John of murdering Arthur than he hears of the arrival of a massive French invasion force bent on overthrowing him, his mother's death, and the almost certain loss of the French lands that she had guarded for England from Philip. Next, the Bastard brings in a prophet who has been telling people that the king would deliver up his crown before the next Ascension Day. As John sends the Bastard away to plead with the angry peers, saying he has "a way to win their loves again," Hubert takes the false prophet off for punishment before returning to report a strange astronomical spectacle and how the common folk connect it to Arthur's death. Consumed with guilt and anger at how his report of Arthur's death was received, John blames him for the killing, saying that his humor was wrongly taken by Hubert for a command. When shown the signed death warrant, John then faults him for not voicing disapproval. Hubert's looks, as "a fellow by the hand of Nature marked, quoted, and signed to do a deed of shame," as John now says, put the idea in his mind.

Hubert's appearance, like Arthur's, has significance in a play so much about disparities between inner and outer, body versus soul, and legitimate against illegitimate. Just as *Coeur de Lion* did not have the outward aspect of a war-loving sociopath, and John looked unheroic, Hubert seems to be a villain; we just have to think of how Prince John is portrayed today, whether in musicals about Lion Kings or cartoons of Robin Hood. Arthur and Richard had never really been in England, and could thus be fitted easily into archetypal slots, the one as Jesus and the other as warlord messiah. John is left evil Herod's role. He does not look like a French lily or a golden Plantagenet, but this does not make him illegitimate, as the barons imply. While the Roman Church worships false appearances and makes ritual into substance, and while Puritans claim to abjure all ritual but worship the surface meaning of an ill-translated text, Christian kingship requires a dramatic path by which deceptive disjunctions of world, flesh, and devil are overcome.

In the world outside the play, Hubert may well have resembled Queen Elizabeth's trusted confidante and spymaster, hunchbacked Sir Robert Cecil, whom she blamed for the execution of the properly signed death warrant to behead her cousin: ex-Queen Mary Stuart. In this famous case, as in those of Archbishop Beckett and Prince Arthur, we have plausible deniability accompanied by suitable displays of royal outrage and remorse. But yet King John is not as skilled an actor as Henry II or Queen Elizabeth were, and maybe his court is more treacherous and less patriotic. But what matters most is that thanks to the well-intentioned but disastrous management of the physical whereabouts of Arthur, all the evidence points towards John. Hubert's act of mercy may have saved John's soul, since the king's relief at hearing that Hubert spared Arthur seems genuine, but it has deeply compromised John's political prospects.

Back in *King John*, maligned Hubert now defends himself and corrects John. He is a liar but not a murderer; the first involves but a white lie, the other a black sin. Telling John that a murderous thought has never entered his heart, Hubert accuses John of having "slandered nature in my form." Once more we find that sin's origin is in the mind rather the body, no matter how beautiful or ugly it may be. It is a spiritually ugly man who wickedly projects or violently imposes his soul's evil intent on the body of another. However rude Hubert's exterior, it is "the cover of a fairer mind than to be butcher of an innocent child." Hubert has defended his body and also all but accused John's mind of great evil.

To John's credit, he apologizes, "Forgive the comment that my passion made upon thy feature, for my rage was blind and foul imaginary eyes of blood presented thee more hideous than thou art." Even if Hubert is "hideous," the real ugliness was imputed to him by John's foul "eyes of blood." Is this way of seeing things through the eyes of Cain a hereditary trait? If so how is Arthur immune from it? And if not, can it be that only murderers see this way?

Though John "only" committed the deadly sin of murder in his heart, and tried to keep his hands clean, he must now take responsibility for what he's done to his murderous agents and his victims. This admission may be the first step on the path to atonement John must take. Hubert did say that he would "make a peace between your soul and you."

But John's first, partially selfish, priority is to send Hubert speedily off to the "incensed peers" to make them "tame to their obedience" by revealing Arthur alive and unharmed. But things do not go as they should. Saying, "As good to die and go as die and stay," Arthur decides to escape the place where he is held, probably Hubert's castle, and jumps down from the wall disguised as a ship-boy. Though he is not putting God to the test, no angels appear to bear him up and the poor little boy falls to his death. His last words, "my uncle's spirit is in these stones, Heaven take my soul, and England keep my bones!" echo Jesus' "Father to thy hands I commend my spirit" as much as his words before leaping resemble "Lord why hast thou forsaken me?" His fate shows he is not the messiah/warlord the age asks for. Arthur, despite his childlike wisdom, is too frail and gentle for the vicious commodious ethos of the time. His garb suggests that he is trying to escape overseas. Arthur may be trying to save Hubert from John's rage. But he may also be trying to save England and France from a new series of wars waged in his name: Would Jesus have endorsed the Crusades?

Meanwhile Salisbury and Pembroke joined by Bigot arrive at the "prison," probably Hubert's castle, where Arthur is held. They discuss an imminent meeting with Lewis, arranged by Pandulph, and it is implied that selfish concerns move them: "It is our safety, and we must embrace this gentle offer of a perilous time." Salisbury seeks to convince the others that Lewis' intentions are more generous than his cagy words. Since we will find that Hubert only left Arthur an hour ago, before giving the false news to John of his death, it is clear that they had made treasonous contact with Lewis before knowing for certain that Arthur had died. This is when the Bastard catches up with them to convey John's urgent summons to meet with him at once. The Barons rudely reject John's authority, Salisbury proclaiming "our griefs and not our manners reason now." But saying of the king that his foot "leaves a print of blood wherever it walks" is a weak excuse; even if Arthur is dead, he is the only victim of the bloody tyranny they allege. Pembroke's empty claim that impatience justifies this rude conduct virtually admits the existence of other reasons behind it. Otherwise they could surely return to the king in high indignation after finding

51

Arthur's body. But while that was the reason given for leaving John's court, their conduct after finding the boy dead is very suggestive.

Also noteworthy is the extravagant language employed by the three barons when Arthur's body is found. It recalls the language used in the US after 9/11, or the Roman Church's exclusive concern with the death of Christ and its glaring neglect of all of Rome's other victims and even Jesus' teachings. In short, we cannot forget that while the scene is terribly pathetic, it should surely occasion at least as much suspicion as hyperbole. Why has Arthur's body been so rudely treated? And by whom? It seems that the barons wish only to exploit the situation, not to explain it. In language far more extreme than in *The Troublesome Reign of King John*, Salisbury hysterically rants, "this is the very top, the height, the crest, or crest unto the crest, of murder's arms." Pembroke then piously proclaims to posterity, "All murders past do stand excused in this. And this, so sole and unmatchable, shall give a holiness, a purity, to the yet unbegotten sin of times." More genuinely shocked by the spectacle than either peer, the Bastard is yet more measured. He calls it "a damned and bloody work … if that be the work of any hand," rightly refusing to rule out the possibility of accident. Lacking an agenda, he does not immediately join the peers in blaming Hubert or vowing revenge on John.

Hubert now comes on the scene, "hot with haste," to tell the Barons: "Arthur doth live; the King has sent for you." It can only be after saying these words that he sees the body; it is striking that he is left speechless by the sight, all the more when this response is contrasted to the prepared prolixity of the peers. He will claim to have left Arthur alive an hour ago, when he departed for court; and if this is true he could not have returned to kill Arthur since the barons left before him, but this alibi is tainted by his publicly having told John that Arthur was dead. Any effort at defending himself and explaining this falsehood would only discredit John. While the peers accept his excuse in *The Troublesome Reign of King John*, especially since he has a chance to tell them that he deceived the king to temper his wrath, and they prefer to pin the act on John's minions acting under orders, in *King John* they are most adamant in claiming that John and Hubert acted in concert. The Bard alters *King John* so the Bastard can defend Hubert against the Barons' wish to scapegoat him without any inquiry.

The Bastard, who has been made Duke of Normandy in *The Troublesome Reign of King John*, but remains Sir Richard in *King John*, stands up to

Salisbury after the latter draws on Hubert, who then unsheathes his own sword to defend itself. While Bigot calls Hubert a "dunghill" and asks if he dares to defy or challenge a nobleman, Hubert contends that he will defend his innocence even before an emperor. When Pembroke demands that he be cut to pieces for daring to accuse a nobleman of lying, and Salisbury then threatens the Bastard for asking him to "keep the peace," the Bastard replies contemptuously by threatening to "maul" him and his "toasting iron." He implies that Salisbury, a fellow royal bastard, who gained his title by being married by Richard to a rich child heiress, is unworthy of both his sobriquet "Longsword" and his title. *King John* even mischievously disparages the virtue of Pembroke, also known as William the Marshall; in spite of his great renown as a soldier, the Marshall also fell out with John over his French lands for which he paid homage to Philip.

Now Hubert again denies killing Arthur; weeping over the loss of the Prince's life, he swears to have "left him well" less than an hour ago. But the Barons refuse to credit this, partially because of his previous false statement to John and also since they wish to join the Dauphin. Publicly announcing their treachery, they ask that John be informed. We see that they are too craven to fight; commodity calls them elsewhere. Even though they had earlier claimed that Arthur's death was the most heinous crime ever, these noble lords will not fight for his mortal remains; there is no need for Hubert and the Bastard to battle them for his body as the Greeks did for Patroclus. But now the Bastard must tell Hubert in the sternest language that he is damned beyond all mercy, more surely than Lucifer, if he killed or consented to the killing of Arthur. Hubert now formally denies that he "in act, consent, or sin of thought" was guilty of this crime, reaffirming that he "left him well." Luckily for John, he does not go into why he falsely told the king of Arthur's death or mention that John had charged him with realizing it. If John can deny fully intending this, so too may Hubert. Luckily for us all, two great abysses separate human wishes, words and deeds from each other. This tripartite order is even found in John's craven distinction between our unspoken thoughts, manifest signs and deliberate deeds; its archetype is the Christian Trinitarian model of the relation of divine ego, logos and activity.

Act IV ends with Hubert taking Arthur's body away as the Bastard reflects on what has happened. Now that Arthur is dead and England's "light, right and truth" are "fled to heaven," John has lost also his own legitimacy—probably by that wicked order but perhaps because he never had it. England is now a bastard realm; what was sacred is lost and its crown is a blanched bone for snarling mongrels to fight over. Meanwhile the Bastard, who behaved splendidly in this crisis, sees that he still has a lot of growing up to do. He is now England's spirit, but its current son-in-law is Lewis, and John is yet the father of the heir. As chance and contumacy play catch with the crown, the Bastard has to be England's conscience amidst the chaos, until a sense of common good, uniting its nobility and natives, is gained.

"There is no sure foundation set on blood": John's words stay with us as we study Act V of *King John*. Murder and lineage, the two meanings of "blood" jostle mercilessly as the Angevin empire collapses around its last king. Does lineage necessarily involve murder to protect one's own? And does it also lead men to slay their own heirs in paranoid fear? Murder seems to leave its own lineage or trail of blood, one that leads us to visit grave damage on our own souls even as we send the bodies of others to their graves. But what then is the foundation of a just political order? The human association where people try to bring out the best in each other, a polity, is said to originate in the family; but it seems that blood, the basis of a family, gives birth to the very vices we try to defeat when we seek a just city. The last act of *King John* begins with John ratifying in deed the moral bankruptcy the Bastard saw summed up in Arthur's death.

By surrendering England to the papacy and receiving it back as a papal fiefdom, John is seen to be indulging in the kind of commodious trickery that sparked the Reformation. Simony, the sale of what is sacred, is what he has done. John has no right to give or sell, *qua object*, what cannot be owned, bought or sold. It is sinful to treat spiritual or political entities in this manner. And yet John has sold the soul of England to preserve his kingship; he may argue that it was in the same pragmatic spirit that he ordered Arthur's killing; he sought to save England from another ugly round of internecine anarchy. Was Caiaphas wrong to defer for a generation the awful war that destroyed Jerusalem?

A nation is an assembly of people, an *ekklesia*, united by a common origin, language and history: a logos. In this spirit they work together towards a common good. This order reflects the trinitarian structure we noted earlier: It is a spiritual entity that cannot be commodified, as

Pandulph and John tried to do. The flawed logic in this vain attempt at re-verse-transubstantiation is seen in their inability to make Lewis call off his invasion. Once the infallible papacy reverses itself, it reveals the essentially arbitrary and volitional character of its power. While it is possible for one false spiritual body or *ekklesia*, the Church, to expose another, a kingdom, and *vice versa*, it is not possible to reduce a polity to a kingdom, a soul to a body, or a true church/*ekklesia* to a commodified religious tribe or bound herd.

It is in this spirit, anticipating Polonius' advice to Laertes, that the Bastard made his famous speech about England being true to itself. The *ekkle-sia*-like polis and soul stands and falls by self-knowledge. This is the *Evangelion*, the word of God to man, reported by Jesus his *logos*, that God is loving and gives grace to the weak and powerless. This news liberates us from (a) the fear of a jealous God who reaps where he does not sow and (b) a Satanic hatred of the self, derived from the doctrine of original sin. This makes self-knowledge a sin of pride against an angry God who knows us better than we know ourselves. The Church claims to have inherited this power via Peter and it knows us as depraved sinners. The stated goal of theocracy is to punish sin and instill purity. It does not try to cultivate virtue in a polis. Even if a true polity could not exist in John's time, one could yet think of the common good; but it seems that John does not, and neither do Lewis, Pandulph or the Barons. Only the Bastard seems to have this end in mind.

If true legitimacy comes from a soul's attention to the common good, it is not passed on through the body and blood lines; as we shall see in *Julius Caesar*, only sin, evil and fury are inherited through blood. In so far as the Church sanctions this legitimacy of blood, it is justified by seeing govern-ment's goal as limiting vice and punishing sin. It is by the sins of the ruler that the sins of the ruled are punished; their fear of him curbs their deprav-ity. Augustine says it is better to be a slave than a master because a slave has less pride and reduced opportunity to sin and anger God. Thus, by sub-mitting to Rome, John has repudiated the idea of founding his throne on blood; but he may also have denied England's common good by surren-dering to Rome and asking relegitimization from the papacy. It is most ironic that where the Church uses its power to bind, it cannot loosen; and when it loosens it cannot rebind; it seems almost as if once these acts of binding and loosening are performed on earth, they are irreversibly ratified in heaven!

It would seem that John's craven submission to Rome was linked to his (wrongly) thinking Arthur to be still alive. Would he have done so if he knew that the alternative was Lewis not Arthur? When the Bastard tells him Hubert was mistaken, and urges John to fight Lewis, he is disgusted to find that John has already submitted to Rome and expects peace to come from this. Urging John to take arms, at least to show France that England does not expect the pope to fight her battles, he is given charge of this "defense." In the absence of the turncoat nobles, slight commodity-driven men, manifestly lacking ancestral courage they claim to have inherited, it seems to be up to the bastards to save the day. Yet we must recall that John, unlike the Bastard, has seen plenty of strife and war; even if he is not Falstaff to the Bastard's Hal, John "soft-sword" has a point. A good king must not be afraid to choose a nation's peace over his honor. This was why his original treaty with Philip was good for England; it only returned lands that were really French to France without bloodshed. *Coeur de Lion* would never have done this; but there is middle ground between being a slack-sword at home and waging endless and costly campaigns abroad for Rome and the Angevin empire.

Meanwhile, in the French camp, we see a strange parody of the Magna Carta being played out. Lewis gives the English defectors written assurances concerning a political compact they have mutually entered into. This agreement was given papal ratification when they took communion at a Mass that Cardinal Pandulph had presided over. It is worth noting here that the news of Arthur's death following Eleanor's led to the loss of Brittany and the Angevin lands. This agreement with Lewis presumably secured the estates of these peers in areas no longer ruled by England. But once this protocol is fully ratified, a few crocodile tears are shed by the English barons: "sons and children of this isle." While claiming to take arms against England with a heavy heart, they give no real reasons for the extraordinary act of taking arms against a king to whom they swore allegiance days ago. Their language is sadly eloquent and poetic but extremely vague and evasive. This is because they have no real evidence that John slew Arthur, as much proof as Hamlet had for proceeding against Claudius; Pembroke admitted as much, when he told the Bastard earlier that haste (to meet with Lewis) was their best reason for refusing to have further speech with John. And they wish that England and France could defy the sea and become one land. Shakespeare's audience would have been aroused by this!

Lewis responds to their hypocrisy with extraordinary unction; it is clear to him that he is dealing with traitors. The rebel peers are marked by frustrated ambitions and itchy palms rather than prophetic souls and tender consciences. Promising Salisbury that he shall thrust his hand "deep into the purse of rich prosperity," a commodious pledge, condescending Lewis urges him to wipe his baby-like tears away. Then, as Pandulph arrives, the Dauphin calls him "angel," equating French gold coins with divine grace. Lewis hints that the Church has been bought off by French gold. Yet Pandulph disappoints Lewis by announcing triumphantly that John has been reconciled to Rome. He calls on Lewis to wind up his "threatening colors" and "tame the savage spirit of wild war" so it may lie gently at the feet of peace.

This Lewis flatly refuses to do: "I am too high born to be propertied, to be a secondary at control, or useful serving state or instrument." War and honor are for him intrinsic parts of the great continuum of commodity. Rome may have "first kindled the dead coals of war," but now the quarrel is his—even if the bond to its origin or cause no longer exists. This is a fine example of the exponential logic of necessity and repetition that takes on a life of its own. The first cause, however hypocritically mouthed, has served its purpose; it is now replaced by the efficient causality of glory. Revived by Peter, Mars has taken the field: "Have I not the best cards for the game, to win this easy match played for a crown. And shall I give over the yielded set? No, no, on my soul, it shall never be said." Soul to him is *thumos*. Though Pandulph, his Pander, vainly protests that he looks "but on the outside of this work," Lewis is firm: "outside or inside, I will not return till my attempt so much be glorified as to my ample hope was promised." The best way to end a war is never to begin one, but John and the Bastard must defend England from an invasion already under way.

When the Bastard arrives to see if Pandulph had succeeded in ending the conflict, he is told that Lewis refuses to lay his arms down. Eager for glory in a worthy cause, the Bastard welcomes this. Richard's son will become Arthur II, the warlord savior of Britain. Lewis likewise has parleyed his wife's Angevin blood into a chance to surpass Henry II. Neither youth is fully aware of the terrible cost of glory. As a result, they now stand poised to tear England apart. The Bard's opinion of the effects of their interaction is clear. The Bastard goes from being a sardonic observer to a jingoistic buffoon; he descends to Lewis' level. Then, when even words fail him, he picks on an image of drumming used by Lewis and the two, sounding more and more like Tweedledum and Tweedledee, try to drum each other out.

Meanwhile, as King John is taken ill with high fever and taken to Swinestead, news comes in that the ships carrying supplies for the French invading force have been wrecked. Before either army has word of this, a badly wounded French lord warns the English barons, fighting against John in betrayal of their coronation oath to him, that Lewis has now sworn, on the very altar where the French and English rebels earlier pledged undying love and amity, to kill them right after his victory. He swears he speaks the truth, for dying men do not need to lie. This makes Salisbury, Pembroke and Bigot "untread" their steps and "return to our great King John." There is also some calculation here since the barons have earlier noted how well "that misbegotten devil," the Bastard, and John's unexpectedly large number of friends fight. While the French still seem to hold the edge, this changing of sides will affect the outcome.

Proud at driving John from the field and making the English retreat at the end of a bloody day's battle, Lewis now hears of the loss of his supply train and the return of his English allies to John. The Dauphin is crestfallen but yet resolved to continue the fight. He does not know that the English are dealing with two worse catastrophes: Even while King John was poisoned and is close to death, half the English army was drowned when the tide unexpectedly came in.

It seems as if the Bastard's own power is diminishing since the barons are reconciled to John. Also, we find out about John's heir, Prince Henry, who appears to replace Arthur. It was at his request that the Barons were pardoned. This news does not please the Bastard; asking God to stay his divine indignation towards the traitors, he hastens to John's side. The implication is that divine anger at the incorporation of the disloyal lords has divided England against itself again, effectively reducing her strength; this anticipates the many civil wars of Henry III's reign. In short, mindless or greedy quantitative accumulation does more harm than good over the long run. Thus, when Salisbury urges Henry to "set a form on that indigest (John) has left so shapeless and so rude," we suspect that this will be at the expense of the "misbegotten" forces that defended England from Lewis and the barons. Hidden modes of commodification will be deployed in the name of God and tradition by selfish bishops and barons, and any call for candid conversation about the common good in a contingent world will be deemed seditious and blasphemous.

As the dying king is brought out to an orchard, prefiguring Richard II, we have three strong hints that the truth about John will not be adequately represented to posterity. Firstly, he was said to have been poisoned by a monk; this is metaphorically, literally the case. The priests and monks on whom we depend for histories or chronicles of his time take a very dim view of this most anti-clerical of kings. For example, Matthew Paris says that "Hell itself is defiled by the presence of John." Secondly, it seems also that Prince Henry and the pardoned traitors around John (Hubert is not with them) believe him to be out of his mind; the Prince talks of his "idle comments," and says the king "rages" or raves, when Holinshed speaks only of John's "anguish of mind." Yet Pembroke, departing, says that John is more patient after the Prince left him, "even now he sung." Thirdly, and most decisively, John says of himself, "I am a scribbled form, drawn with a pen upon a parchment, and against this fire do I shrink up." But as John believes that he is poisoned, and since his fever's symptoms burn in him, his words could be both literally *and* figuratively true.

John clearly has much to be guilty about, especially if he is judged by the monstrously irrational religious norms of the day. But there is something sickening about Richard dying as a hero, with the far lighter conscience, when his sins far exceed those which could be attributed to his brother; John must not be blamed for trying to douse fires lit by Richard. But what is John's own story? There are not many plays like *King John* where the title character does not speak the most words, never reveals his own thoughts to us and does not appear alone on stage. The Bard repeats this trick in *Julius Caesar*, but while his Caesar knows that he is world-renowned, John of *King John* must feel he is always misunderstood. It is up to us to grasp why *Julius Caesar*'s John, who differs greatly from the John of history, legend, and *The Troublesome Reign of King John*, acted as he did. Any true grasp of what Shakespeare seeks to teach and depict through *King John* is only possible after we get a handle on John.

Shakespeare, himself called the Swan of Avon, shows familiarity in *King John* with Socrates' claim in Plato's *Phaedo* that harsh-toned swans begin to sing sweetly and prophetically as they move to their death. John was notorious for his harshness. But what would he have said to us about his life, his accomplishments and his intentions? What would his prophetic swan song be? John had to deal with many adverse conditions and much bad luck. But may he justly claim to have made sweet use of adversity? Even if he did not benefit personally or gain glory, as Richard did, did he serve England well? But to answer this we must study if John's reign changed England, and whether he altered England's awareness of itself. And the best insight here is gained by looking at the Bard's story of the Bastard. Like his alleged father, the prodigal Bastard gave up his lands, changed his name, and followed Eleanor to wage wars overseas.

The Bastard's prophetic words at *King John's* conclusion are made from a position of honor. By tradition, a play's final speaker sums up its meaning and often even represents the dramatist himself. But so much of *King John,* as we just noted, is a story of, and background to, the Bastard's almost novelistic progress in self-knowledge. Like Rosalind's traveler in *As You Like It,* he comes to us at play's end with rich eyes and empty hands. As sharers in the theatre's gift economy, we learn to see, and profit, by seeing reality through his eyes; we then reward him with the applause of grateful hands. We too have been relieved of many illusions, much false wealth, and find ourselves in possession of self-knowledge.

The Bastard stands for the Bard's defense of the integrity of the soul, the nation, and the cosmos. The contrary ideas of original sin, empire and creation—for this is the political theology of a jealous God with absolute right over all he has made out of nothing—place us in the false fetters of theocratic necessity; Augustinian predestination and Hobbes' mechanistic Ananke ultimately affirm the same worldview. *King John* offers a bastard soul redemption from the clerically crafted chains that suspend human consciousness over a mad chaotic abyss. This prospect of a living death without any control over one's own thoughts was Hamlet's greatest nightmare: the cause of his bad dreams. And yet the full force of Augustine's idea of a God within us, the belief in an angry accusing deity who, *qua* creator, knows us better than we can know ourselves, polluted the knowledge-deprived mind of mediaeval man in a way we can only call Satanic. Neither must we discount the negative way the ignorant relate to other; each convinced they know less than their predecessors and peers, but determined to hide this insecurity from peers, peons and progeny.

But what has the Bastard learned? His character, as noted before, is that of a prodigal son. Having sold his lands, and gone abroad in search of fame and fortune, he found—like Touchstone—that the manners of court and commodity sit badly on both conscience and country. He then battled bravely for England in a way that would quite baffle Henry V. He has looked deep into the abyss but only seen much evidence of commodious corruption, no proof of original sin. Evil comes from ambitious parents, needless wars, selfish nobles and power-hungry priests, not from a basic flaw in our nature. Sacred bloodlines, property rights, clerical codes, and aristocratic privileges are ways of hiding evil; they conceal the basic truth that human souls are not superior or inferior to each other by birth; thus "as sure as night follows day," the right to be true to oneself or seek truth for oneself cannot be denied yet must always be fought for.

Despite extended exposure to the many evils pervading church and state, matters that would lead to the Reformation and Enlightenment but not be rectified fully by either, the Bastard has profited from his experiences. Disenchanted, but not neither nihilistic nor cynical, his resilient spirit somehow survives; he continues to believe in England and virtues that avert the false choice between the casuistic Catholicism of the past and the cruel Calvinism that looms ahead. Though saddened by the reemergence of old evils in Henry III's court, he can leave the stage convinced that some progress has been made. Decisively separated from Europe, England has come to exist as a nation state, and opportunities for new men like Hubert and himself will increase as English becomes the language of state. Even the Church, unreformed for three more centuries, will slowly feel its wings clipped as secular forces of nationalism and literacy query Rome's right to use crusades, interdicts, inquisitions and excommunications to tyrannize human souls.

Complementing the freedom Paul proclaims in Galatians from the impossible demands of Mosaic Law that makes angry guilty sinners of us all, the good news of King John's Gospel according to his Bard is that we are all bastards and thus emancipated from our Holy Father. England became an illegitimate nation by its physical separation from Europe, its ecclesiastic divorce from Rome, and its intellectual rejection of the scholastic tradition. Clerical accounts of original sin, and the Catholic intellectual tradition itself are corrupted by commodity. Rome's "usurped authority" is profaned by its own hypocrisy; its sacred rituals and profane priests merely seek commodious advantage, instead of binding us to our sacred origins as they claim. Cloaking its self-righteous malice as Petrine care, papal clericalism stresses God's jealous nature, hence the need for ritual. But this makes God cruel and corrupt in himself, as he both uses and corrupts humans. Being declared a bastard or heretic leads us from these temptations and delivers us from evil. Elizabeth was seen as a bastard until becoming Queen and had now been excommunicated for as many years.

The Bastard's closing speech rejoices that the separation of England and France is complete, and the rift between barons and Britons is healed: "Naught shall make us rue, if England to itself do rest but true." As the sea gives safety from the see of Peter, it lets England be true to itself. The greatest peril, as with Israel, is for this "holy nation and people set apart" to imitate or merge with other nations. It must never "help to wound itself" again. England must trust in its own land, arms, people, church, and tongue. John deserves credit for his strategic withdrawal from Empire; his last thought was of the safety of the land. The Bastard mourns John's death but rejoices that England "never did, and never shall lie at the proud foot of a conqueror." Is this not also part of his tribute to John? How did John do this?

The significance of the burning heat John felt on his deathbed could be traced back to his prophetic anger at Rome when Philip was made by Pandulph to betray their treaty. The Bastard's words complement those of Hugh Latimer, Bishop of Worcester, John's gravesite, as Mary burned him at the stake a quarter millennium later, "we shall this day light such a candle, by God's grace, in England, as I trust shall never be put out." The Bastard adds, "Come the three corners of the world in arms, and we shall shock them." John lit three fires and suffered three defeats at the hands of the Church, France, and the Barons. But the flame of his anger never gave out in the Bastard's England. This fire fuels resistance and stoked enduring outrage from England's own corner towards the other three. The three eventual results were Protestantism, prudent patriotism, and parliamentary democracy. John's defeats contributed far more than the famous but Pyrrhic victories of Richard, Edward I, Edward III or Henry V to the English Constitution.

But who will turn John's fevered Viking/pagan deathbed into these three progressive causes? Henry III was far too pious, willing to fight French wars and obedient to barons. The Bard himself did much to help bring this about. He undertook an English transformation of Greek tragedy; what oligarchic Rome added to muzzle and domesticate this political genre was removed. We can still see hints of a Greek spirit of tragic defiance in the English love of doomed rearguard actions and honorable defeat; a people learn more, and are united spiritually, by noble sorrow in a way far more profound than anything achieved by the animalistic ecstasy of hubristic victory. Signifying a rejection of both commodious comedy and the rapturous rage of a revenge play, *King John* is the Bard's only English tragedy beside *Lear*.

Both John and Lear are angry kings, but the causes and results of the two respective choleric states cannot be more different. While Lear's rage is chthonic, John's anger is that of a founder; it was the condition for the possibility of future advances, some unthinkable in the day of either the historical figure or his character. By taking on the Church and willy-nilly separating England from Europe, John gave voice to a collective anger that would let his country start seeing itself as a commonwealth, lead to the English Reformation, and slowly allow all of its people to participate in deciding the common good. Shakespeare is not only the great tragic muse of Modernity; the Bard was also formed by the very chthonic powers he employed to such sublime effect in resurrecting true tragedy from the old turgid genre of revenge plays. In short, the Bard himself came from this process and he now contributes to it. His character King John could be seen as part historical figure and part personification of this collective progress. Even if this John never was, he was real to the extent of helping to produce Shakespeare: the poet who created him. Shakespeare's John is also a stand-in for the Bard's father, John Shakespeare.

Written around the same time as the comedy *As You Like It*, and complementing its gentle mockery of prelapsarian myth and fairy tale endings, *King John* gives England an anti-foundational founding myth. Instead of desperately trying to maintain sacred links to a literally Romanticized past in a way that denigrates and denies the present, the Bard shows us how poetic history can augment our ability to love the present. Just as in *As You Like It*, Rosalind, the Duke's cast-off daughter, brings her father back from his fake Eden to re-found his dukedom, the Bastard helps John to move from a code of commodity (actually preferred over the predatorial psychopathy of Richard and many barons) and become the first true king of England since before the Conquest. As with *As You Like It*, this anti-foundational founding enhances our ability to see the full richness of an otherwise reified reality. Even if virtue of this kind may well be short-lived, and is very susceptible to priestly poison and plutocratic predation, it still preserves the—necessarily vulnerable—three candles of Patriotism, Protestantism, and Parliament, first lit in England by Shakespeare's imperfect founder: King John.

Just as prudent patriotism jealously defends the integrity of England from alien power, but also saves her people from needless and costly foreign wars or Crusades that only serve the pride and greed of the ambitious, Protestantism will defend Jesus' words against vain papal bulls. And parliament, which placed his subjects over the monarch a century after *King John*, will fight to protect all Britons and their rights from power-hungry bishops and barons. These very English negative triumphs also accept imperfection; we must never forget that Lackland is better for Britain than Lionheart.

More positively, we may talk of how lordship, land and language are defined in *King John*. A meddling pope is replaced by a king as sovereign of England. His realm is not imperial or otherworldly but "Little England." And English will not only replace French as the language of rule, but also be used by Englishmen to discuss their common good together. It is also necessary to see how these three themes are as urgent in *King John*'s time as in King John's. Anglicanism requires England to steer a *via media* between Papal and Puritan currents; spirited nobles must be deterred from costly Irish wars, and made to think of England first; and Parliament must deal with an autocratic ruler and no firm succession. This is why *King John*'s basic motif, the intellectual, spiritual and moral benefits of being a bastard, is of great importance.

In any time, including our own, when alienation abounds and souls are trapped in a mad Aspergian or Kafkaesque labyrinth of sacred rules and rituals, no longer making sense to anyone but followed with obsequious diligence, the desire to leave civilization and be an outlaw is perfectly logical. While the Bard gave this topic comic treatment in *As You Like It*, we have suggested that *King John* offers a more esoteric account of this dangerous topic. While the usual response to this frustration takes some form of saying "there is no salvation outside the Church," and uses some form of original sin to justify itself, we may be correct in saying that the true original sin is the desire to trust in our fabulous origins and deny the soul any power or right to see or say what is self-evident. As we noted, the basis for this stance is the claim of rulers to be divinely anointed to see through God's eyes, and thus know us better than we can know ourselves. They usually deny that it is power rather than right that makes them shameless or foolish enough to make these claims, but it matters little if a man with a gun to your head obeys an inner master or just feels like it. But it is scarier when victims feel they have no choice but to obey. They would rather die than be impious or illogical; even uglier than the banality of evil is the pusillanimity of a victim who dies saying that everything happens for a reason.

John and the Bastard embody the political and personal meanings of illegitimacy. If all law is posited from beyond us, then either by this fact, or by acquiescing in it, humans live in a dark Hades without benefit of reason; we are natural slaves. Yet the action of *King John* shows that it is possible to overcome this self-imposed blindness, and then take steps to free others from it; even if the results may be tragic, this is still better than a long sad life of blind servitude. If the subtext of the Prodigal Son means anything at all, the Father is surely more pleased with those who search for their destiny; using Pharisaic obedience to be tied to a God "who will be what he will be" is a kind of blasphemy. That is why this chapter concludes by studying the implications of the bastard or outlaw ethics *King John* points towards.

If we are rational animals, to be human is to see life through our own eyes and never allow others to think for us. And if we are political animals, then we must live in cities where we are free(d) to discuss the beautiful and just. To maim ourselves like Oedipus, refusing to be anything other than blind soulless solipsistic shadows, is not tragedy but infernal comedy; it is surely a great impiety against our nature and its maker. This is why the Bastard must uproot himself from his false origins. It is also what makes John repudiate his Angevin heritage and defy the pope. In each case, chains of legalistic reasoning that bind soul and country to sacred but dubious origins are rejected at the cost of legitimacy; while the Bastard sacrifices a commodious life to discover his heroic soul, *King John*'s John braves the wrath of Rome and his barons, and even lets his own legitimacy be questioned, so England may be true to her pagan soul.

This stress on the present, living in reality and not piously tying oneself to shadows, has large philosophic and legal implications. Medieval society's view of truth in terms of blood-lines and legitimacy, where parents tried to transmit property to their children and ended up reifying themselves and making their offspring property to be bred, bought and sold, began with the Romans. Before this, souls and the gods they worshipped may have been seen in speech, deeds and influence on others in the polis. But this ended when Rome replaced politics with economics. Worship of the Emperor, family, and private property delegitimized Greek politics and its deliberation about justice and beauty.

Living beyond Roman law, outlaws and bastards recover Arcadia; here love of justice and beauty override occult origins and rage for order. Exempted by Socratic ignorance from indebtedness to angry ancestors, whose ways must be imitated, and jealous gods demanding punctilious performance of obscure rituals, they live in a pre-fallen world. True virtue comes from erotic attraction to what is best in the world, and it is directed towards the other, the weak and vulnerable; Hubert did not spare Arthur because Christ died for his sins. Goodness is not based on an otherworldly perfection that is mimed with self-effacing humility or soul-numbing self-hatred. But while true virtue cannot be imposed on any soul, most of us voluntarily link ourselves to false chains of reasoning, by ignorance, prejudice, habit or inertia. In such cases, the best one can do is to model what virtue looks like and show how it leads to happiness.

The next best thing is to contain impulses towards evil in us and ensure that they do not pass to the next generation; even if John treated Arthur badly, we must yet give him credit for not poisoning Prince Henry with a fury-driven desire to avenge him. John's words, "within me is a hell, and there the poison is as a fiend confined to tyrannize on irretrievable condemned blood," point towards issues that confront us in *Julius Caesar* and *Hamlet*. But we must note that the dying king has won a huge psychic victory by not giving in to this temptation and passing on his terrible Plantagenet temper to his heirs. He is a founder, not a role model, only to be imitated in his care for the unity and security of England. He would rather be silently honored for this achievement than loved by a divisive faction.

The lion-hearted Bastard must surely recognize this as well. He also sees, as does John, that with depleted forces he is in no position to contest the ascendency of the rebel peers. Past scores must be set aside for the sake of unifying England. John and the Bastard must both hope that with their French lands lost and Lewis' murderous intentions revealed, Salisbury and Pembroke will be led by a combination of shame and commodity to serve Henry III loyally. We know from history that this was the case. Meanwhile, the Bastard must recede into the English soil and serve as one of many "unknown soldiers" in this or any successful containment of evil. He embodies a very English heroism. His land, splendidly isolated, does not need any Richards or standing armies rampaging around for the greater glory of God. The Bastard knows that both French invasions were ultimately defeated by England's greatest ally—the sea. Just as land and sea complement and keep each other in check, so too do church and state, like earth and air, also limit the excesses of Empire and Theocratic tyranny; John's fire thus curbs Paul's "prince of the power of the air."

Despite the Second Brexit, *King John*'s message, looking past its spirited content, is that it is by her literature, not by her empire or fleet, that England will continue to civilize. The Bard's Christian humanism does not work by meddling priests or forced conversions. Through him and in his corpus, the Logos of compassion and charity wins more hearts and souls than any Crusade, Conquistador or company ever could. Shakespeare has brought more bastard brothers and sisters together, in shared love and delighted wonder at his humanity, each other's and their own, than any writer since the age of Classical Greece. Wherever two or more are gathered by him, the Logos will be there. The Bard has risen from the corrupt church and narrative of Christianity to recover the erotic essence or "look" of Jesus' gospel.

CHAPTER THREE
THE TRAGEDY OF BRUTUS:
ENVY, HONOR, AND FILIAL FURY IN *JULIUS CAESAR*

This chapter will concern itself with Shakespeare's examination of Brutus' soul. How would noble Brutus have understood himself and his most notable action in the doom-haunted days between deed and downfall? *Julius Caesar* depicts Brutus as trying too hard to be worthy of his noble name and ending up destroyed by a combination of pride, blindness, and the fury of his victim. Shakespeare shows us how, in attempting to preserve the Republic, Brutus brought about its assured destruction. Even more ironically, he is the means by which the zombie-apotheosis of Caesar and triumph of Caesar-ism came about.

Shakespeare seems to give us a key to his take on Marcus Brutus by misquoting Plutarch's *Life of Brutus* in *Julius Caesar*. Just before Brutus dies, cursing Antony and Octavius, he boasts, "I never found man but that he was true to me." Was he not so deceived by Cassius that his very last words were "Caesar now be still, I killed thee not with half so good a will"? Does he not need Polonius' advice to his easily duped son, "above all, to thine own self be true"? Or can it be that Brutus' final words, failing to express any regret for his part in the downfall of the Roman Republic, show us how Shakespeare sees the selfishness, self-deception and solipsism of this fake-Stoic and famously false friend?

Perhaps, but *Julius Caesar's* distortion of Plutarch's words "none of his friends was ever false to him" draws our attention to friendship and its corruption in the oligarchic old order. We must ask if Brutus truly had any friends and go on to speculate over the significance of Antony's "Friends, Romans, countrymen" as opposed to Brutus' "Romans, countrymen and lovers." Did this neglect of friendship contribute to Brutus' prideful lack of self-knowledge and make it possible for him to be badly deceived by both Cassius and Antony in turn, before the angry ghost of Caesar confronted his guilty soul and administered the final coup de grace? In short, how did Brutus see himself and how did this false consciousness cause his fate and doom the Classical Age itself? How is patrician Roman consciousness different from the Greek *sophrosune* that it defeated in war but always felt culturally inferior to? If the answers to (some of) these questions can be seen in Act I of *Julius Caesar*, this could mean we are on the right track. Corroboration of my idea may be had if it helps explain the relation of 1590's Reformation England to Rome, its Church and the West.

The almost irrelevant opening scene of *Julius Caesar* turns out to be of much value when we use it as our key to open up the main theme of this otherwise confusing play, its mostly absent title character, and its enigmatic main protagonist. Our play begins with an incongruous conflict between Rome's commoners and two aristocratic tribunes, their supposed representatives. While the common citizens rejoice in Caesar's triumphs, the tribunes seek to exclude them from the public celebrations and bitterly denounce their supposed ingratitude towards Pompey, the great champion of the Patrician party, whom Caesar has vanquished. But even if Pompey had hitherto provided them with bread and circuses, by securing the Roman grain supply from pirates and giving the mob extravagant public entertainment, surely the people are entitled to celebrate the end of a period of bitter internecine civil war? We note that Pompey was on the side of those who excluded the poor from the deliberative space of the Republic.

The patricians jealously guarded this res-publican right, the power to determine the public good of Rome, deeming it a sacred inheritance from their fathers. It is in this spirit that the Tribune describe the common people as "blocks and stones." The urban rabble are but the rubble or raw material out of which Rome's greatness is fashioned. It is felt absurd that they should presume to have consciousness beyond what is sufficient for obedience or admiration.

If the commoners made up Rome's armies, and waged centuries of "defensive" wars that led to the conquest of the entire Mediterranean world, they never shared in the massive profits that accrued from these campaigns. While most soldiers rarely survived 25 years of military service, and often lost their small farms (that could not be run without them) to the rich, the proud patrician proconsuls commanding these patriotic paupers became colossally wealthy. This was the very cause that led to the Social Wars between the Optimates or Senatorial Party of Sulla, Pompey, Cicero, Cassius and Brutus, and the Populares or party of the people led by Julius Caesar and Antony.

Shakespeare cuts to the chase by punning repeatedly on the homonym that can be spelled as either "sole" or "soul." He seems to play the part of a cobbler—of words or shoes—whose livelihood it is to repair the worn-out leather soles/souls of the Romans. As well as deriving this trade from his own father's business (old John Shakespeare was a maker of leather gloves), this witty character claims disingenuously to drum up custom for himself by urging the common rabble to wear their shoes out following Caesar's triumph. He even offers to fix the worn-out soles and souls of the angry tribunes. Like Shakespeare, he lives by the awl or all, catering to the souls of the all or *demos*. While he must be prudent, for his life and craft are at risk, this irrepressible clown can teach us the very subversive truth that all have souls. It is worthwhile to risk our souls following him through Rome's streets. He can save us all or, at least, show how Western Civilization and the Roman Church ended up where they are after the Reformation.

Julius Caesar is thus a therapeutic exercise for the souls of our Bard's audience; we do not seek exact historic truth of him and neither does he claim to have it. A cobbler cannot be expected to know precisely where the shoes he mends have been. Yet he can shrewdly speculate as to what sort of experiences a certain sole has undergone, and also perform appropriate repairs whenever possible. In short, while both the poet and cobbler derive human wisdom from their wide experience of many souls, their ends have to do with the future rather than the past of those whom they aid. It is thus in this cobbler's company that we move to scene 2 and see the principal protagonists—with the exception of Octavius, yet too young for public life-take the stage. We see the Roman political arena from our cobbler's eyes. Only he can depict men's souls/soles. Our souls are oft' hidden to our eyes, especially if we seek to excel all others.

We first find that the wife of the dictator for life, and thus by extension mighty Rome itself, is unfertile. It is rich but rotted within. Who or what should succeed Caesar's absolute but barren success? The Lupercalia which re-enacts a miracle by which savage nature saved two orphan brothers and set up a city, reminds us of *Julius Caesar's* challenge: The link between Rome's impotent past and indigent future has to be renewed, if only by

70

animal nature, red in tooth and claw. While the suggestion is that fraternal strife is inevitable given the lack of parental authority, we must also see how it is this very patriarchal structure that has spawned the situation in which 44 BC Rome finds itself. It is surely undesirable that the descendants of Romulus and Remus, Optimates and Populares, or Oligarchs and Democrats, must continually fight each other to the death. While defensive wars were once an easy way by which aggressive civic humors were safely conveyed beyond the city, it is now no longer possible for the Roman polity to postpone psychic digestion of what a century of social strife has revealed. A Roman commonwealth or good no longer exists. Corrupted by power, wealth and empire, patricians and plebs have incompatible political interests. The two parties cannot speak truly to each other or among themselves; even worse, good men must struggle to lie to themselves and stay stoically silent before others. A great deal of self-respect is lost in this terribly violent internal conflict. It is impossible to honor sacred patrician values without denying the evident humanity and rights of the plebian many.

After Caesar and his party go to the festival, Cassius is left with his estranged brother-in-law Brutus. Shakespeare leaves out this family tie. He also omits the rumor, noted by Suetonius and attributed to Cicero, that Cassius' wife had been Caesar's mistress. This suggests they are only tied by friendship and a cause, albeit of Cassius' making. He is no jealous Iago. It is also worth noting here that Shakespeare's Brutus is much weaker than the man described by Plutarch. While the *Parallel Lives* portrays an educated middle-Platonist philosopher and successful governor, *Julius Caesar's* Brutus is a would-be Stoic and a Proto-Hamlet. This Brutus is putty in Cassius' hands. When denying Cassius' plaint that he neglects the love due to his friend, feebly claiming to be at war with himself, Brutus is shaken to the core by the charge that his distemper is not personal but political. Claiming to know Brutus better than he knew himself and acting as his midwife, Cassius deftly helps Brutus deliver two conflicting thoughts; using the ominous backdrop of clamor at the Lupercalia to make Brutus' love and gratitude to Caesar seem selfish beside the fear that the aging dictator-for-life would assume the crown itself, he seduces the scion of Junius Brutus to declare his guarded choice to rather be a villager than to remain a Roman under a king. By this, Cassius makes Brutus forsake his claim to care for the general good of all the Romans, which could very well have been better served by Caesar, and focus only on setting his patrician honor above and against the base fear of death *and* concern for the good of the base. As Shakespeare's Falstaff taught Prince Hal, the mad craving for honor is every nobleman's Achilles heel.

Cassius uses various reductive devices to preemptively cut Caesar down to size, contrasting the dictator's aging body to the colossal stature he held in the public imagination, and suggesting that this gross disproportion had the effect of reducing the noblest patricians to the level of mere plebs, begging like clients for favors and positions. While Cassius does not state that this logic could be extended to make all human bodies or souls equal, it is made clear enough that Brutus' ancestral honor would be jeopardized and his own name disgraced if he did not act.

Once Brutus leaves and he is left alone on stage, Cassius, already fingered by Caesar as a "lean and hungry" man who "thinks too much," muses aloud about the susceptibility of even noble men like Brutus to base influence. He thinks Caesar loves Brutus while being ill-disposed towards him. This matches with Plutarch's report that Caesar preferred Brutus over Cassius for the coveted position of Urban Praetor. It seems as if he is moved by feelings that are far different than those lofty feelings of patrician honor he shared with Brutus. Cassius will merely use Brutus to get even with Caesar. Cassius has few illusions about himself; his mind is moved by envy. Believing reality to be ruled by randomness and fortune, he will use fraud and flattery to undermine Brutus' Stoicism. The ugly question of whether Brutus' nobility is true or feigned is left undecided. Cassius himself, *qua* Epicurean, could hardly hold that blood tells if one is divinely blessed; it is but a mark of mortality mutually held by Caesar, Brutus, and brutes.

Despite having reduced names to sounds, Cassius finds the name "Brutus" to be his associate's biggest weakness. Though Caesar's victory has created openings for good men to promote the general good, and the dictator has gone out of his way to prefer Brutus, Cassius persuades Brutus that he will betray his name and ancestral honor by honoring Julius before Junius. The fatalistic Stoic way of doing what was right, regardless of result, bends easily to serve an unconscious ambition that cannot speak its own name. But who would Servilla's son be, if not Brutus? We find that the man known as Marcus Brutus has altered his name many times. Also, that there is a name not taken. Even if *Julius Caesar* does not reveal all Plutarch tells, and its maker had not read Cicero's letters, his Cassius does enough to universalize Brutus' specific insecurities and show how honor's ranting rhetoric may blind any man's conscience.

While Brutus is yet literally Brutus, a brute or man without friends or a city—a "villager" as he puts it—the conspiracy against Caesar promises to make him worthy of his famous ancestor's name. His conscience will be formed, and he himself un-brutalized by the fine, freedom-loving friends drawn around him by Cassius. In reality, they will murder his soul as surely as they will brutalize Caesar's body. According to Antony, Brutus was Caesar's angel; by killing his good angel, Brutus makes Caesar his evil spirit. Antony knows that only the evil men do lives after them. We shall see how the souls of Antony, Brutus, and Octavius, Caesar's favorites, are polluted by his untimely death.

In Brutus' case, Cassius seduced an insecure but generous nature by projecting his self-doubts towards Caesar and turning Brutus into the figurehead for a scheme of vengeance that would almost inevitably consume its instigators. More evidence of Cassius' dark art is seen in his recruitment of Casca to the conspiracy; here we see an angry and superstitious man made to direct all his fear and rage on Caesar. In each instance Caesar is scapegoated for the psychic flaws of his killers. We could say with Cassius that the fault lies not in their victim but in themselves; letting others interpret events for them, the conspirators were duped into playing the hubristic role of heaven's scourge.

Before the faction fully coalesces and the conspiracy takes its final form, Brutus deliberates alone in his orchard. In this suggestively named pre-fallen setting, which also anticipates the under-explained murder of King Hamlet, it is sufficiently clear to him that Caesar has done nothing to deserve assassination. Already possessing absolute power, the dictator for life has given no sign of having been corrupted by it. Brutus on the other hand reasons in darkness and fears the ambitious alter-ego that Cassius has conjured into existence from the depth of his inchoate soul. To the extent that his thought process begins with a result, "it must be by his death," it is seen to be driven by a fallen will, and Brutus' inference that since he has no personal grudge against Caesar, his motivation must stem from a care for the general (good), ignores the distinction between soul and honor Cassius has already craftily exploited. And while those desirous of honor are surely more likely to be corrupted by it than those already possessed of it, Brutus is already so poisoned by this need that he fails to see the lust in his own heart. No wonder he calls for light.

Useful illumination into this need is gained when we look to Plutarch's *Life of Brutus*, Shakespeare's main source, and find that Caesar, who had carried on an affair with Cato's sister and Brutus' mother Servilia for many years might well have been Brutus' real father. Although better informed historians have denied this likelihood on sound chronological grounds unavailable in Shakespeare's time, this nagging suspicion would surely have influenced the character of his Brutus (and Hamlet). The noble Brutus' mother (and parentage) should surely be above suspicion! Yet the deeper we follow this possibility, the more it explains the character of *Julius Caesar's* Brutus. For one thing it explains the peculiar silence he keeps toward his wife, Portia, Cato's daughter. It is not that he cannot trust her to keep a secret. The problem is that his honor, and his mother's, would be besmirched by the very act of sharing these self-doubts, even if they were the subject of patrician gossip. Stoic morality would not tolerate such a falling short.

It would also appear that Caesar's strong partiality towards Brutus, including his preferment over Cassius, could be explained as being occasioned by nepotism rather superiority in virtue. Cassius could easily manipulate him to kill Caesar by implicitly suggesting that any reluctance on Brutus' part would have to do with fear of slaying his father; this can also be seen to parallel Hamlet's hesitation to kill Claudius. What if his mother's lover is his natural father?

It was easier for Junius Brutus, he merely had to kill his sons when they conspired with exiled King Tarquin against the Roman Republic; this was applauded as the ultimate act of civic piety. Marcus Brutus, however, runs the risk of being haunted by the furies of his true father, if he kills Caesar in attempting to prove his right to the name Brutus.

Plutarch provides a final piece of evidence, more than gossip in this case, that strengthens my argument. We find that Brutus took the side of Pompey the Great in the civil war between Caesar and Pompey despite his legal father and Servilia's husband, Marcus Junius Brutus the Elder, having being killed on Pompey's orders. After this his son, our Brutus, temporarily took the name of his adoptive father and maternal uncle Quintus Servilius Caepio Brutus. It would again seem that Marcus Junius Brutus the Younger would not have chosen to side with his father's killer had he not (a) been reluctant to draw attention to the link with Caesar *and* (b) unafraid of his father's furies; both of these conditions would have been met if Caesar had in fact been Marcus Brutus' natural father. We also know that Caesar took precautions to ensure that Brutus should be unharmed after Pompey's defeat. And yet, these favors only deepen Brutus' suspicions, vouchsafed to Cassius, that he is "not himself." To be or not to be Brutus?

Returning to the orchard, we must see that it is this lack of self-knowledge that prevents Brutus from grasping the true import of his own reflections on the danger of power; even Cassius saw that sleepless Brutus needs friends to see his own soul, otherwise invisible to itself. But Cassius, by his own admission, is no true friend to Brutus; he only needs a man of unimpeachable integrity to be the face of his conspiracy. The faceless faction will hail him as Brutus instead of forcing him to ask "what's in a name" of himself. Indeed, Cassius did so, comparing the words "Brutus" and "Caesar," but he did so not to separate Brutus' soul from the honor-giving sound tied to him, but to bind him all the more pridefully and brutishly to it, and the conspiracy. His soul is not what it is "augmented" by the name.

As noted earlier, and before his anonymous but prophetic soul was seduced by forged petitions and the flattery of the faction, the future assassin had already realized that men are changed by power; the preemptive strike aimed at Caesar's already realized ambitions is far better directed towards those who hope to supplant him. In the case of Rome's dictator, "the serpent's egg" has already hatched and the non-venomous kingsnake has done little more than kill other snakes. But after they strike, its killers will point to its colors to hide their evil motives. As with Brutus' name, the problem is not with Caesar becoming "king"—monarch in all but name: He has not done any of the acts he will be killed for being capable of. Caesar's foes are the real danger; they project their own venom on him.

But these sage reflections are interrupted by several missives thrown toward the ego of Brutus. By opening these notes, he will resume his identity with the name and Roman dignity of Brutus. Cassius has shrewdly left out many key words from the attached appeals, thus inviting "the soul that has resumed the persona of Brutus" to fill in the blanks with its own wishes, desire and fears. In so doing, Brutus now aligns his will with that of his tempter; re-dressed as Junius Brutus, and having light from Lucius to complete the persona of his illustrious ancestor, the son of Servilla will "re-dress" the grievances of those asking him to rescue the Roman Republic from a second Tarquin. Even as the sons of the first Brutus were sacrificed for Rome, so too will the father of this Brutus die for the city.

Brutus is still aware that the path he is on is nightmarish. Between the desire to perform a dreadful deed and its performance, the soul passes through a hideously surreal period, a kind of regime change where all its basic morals are first uprooted, seen as arbitrary, and radically un-aligned. Brutus, trying to reconcile integrity and family honor, enters this place of shamelessness. Here, under night's cover, dark matters are decided and done. This dream-world gives us a time to live our darkest fantasies out without dealing with their awful consequences in real time. But Brutus soon crosses this personal Rubicon. Relying on his honor to protect his in-tegrity, he goes to meet the conspirators and encounters a group of men whose faces are as muffled to him as his own intentions are inscrutable to them.

When Cassius continues with his *modus operandi* of telling Brutus that each of those introduced by name wishes that he had the high opinion of himself that "every noble Roman" has of him, it seems that the assembled body of the murderous conspiracy spontaneously animates its troubled head. Carefully desisting from making mention of the ugly action they are assembled to perform, Brutus asks his associates to join their hands together, one by one. Yet, this as much as anything else gives proof of his internal turmoil. Their energy must override his troubled mind.

As the meeting continues, Brutus seems to infuse just enough idealistic virtue and selfish vanity to weaken the conspirators' plan. He first firmly rejects Cassius' proposal that they swear their resolution, most likely because he fears with good reason that their reasons have nothing to do with his, saying that oaths are not needed when high-minded Romans assemble for a virtuous cause. It seems that he is thereby implicitly pledging them to serve noble ends that are unclear to him and probably unattractive to them. But, as their putative leader, Brutus has his way.

This curious pattern persists when Cicero's possible role in their con-spiracy is discussed. Cassius believes that he will "stand strong" with them. But Brutus casts his veto yet again, even after Metellus chimes in support of Cicero, saying that the great orator's age, prudence, and reputation will give gravity and credibility to their relative youth. Brutus promptly rejects this reasoning, claiming that Cicero will never follow anything begun by other men, but perhaps revealing more about his own vanity and uncertainty than showing any insight into Cicero's suitability. He could very well fear that Cicero's intellect and prudence would carry more weight than his own integrity and noble name. Brutus would then be overshadowed among the conspirators. Neither can we forget that Cicero is a *Novus homo*, the first in his family to enter the senate, a man of humble origins. Would this compromise Brutus' honor? But Brutus' view prevails again after the irascible and volatile Casca, whose superstitious attitude toward recent prodigious atmospheric events had just been gently discounted by a skeptical Cicero, also finds him not to be fit. It must also be noted that Cicero was one of those who circulated the rumor that Caesar was Brutus' real father.

But it is when the plotters turn to discuss the fate of Caesar's friend and fellow consul Mark Antony that we see Brutus make his third and greatest error of judgment. As part of his continuing effort to deceive himself about the true nature of their ugly conspiracy, Brutus has attempted to govern it by the highest and most abstract ideals. He would preside over the assassination like a high priest, trying to turn a vicious act of revenge into most holy ritual. Caesar must be killed "boldly but not wrathfully," and "carved up as a dish fit for gods"—not a "carcass for hounds." Accordingly, he rejects Cassius' prudent but bloody proposal that Antony be killed along with Caesar; arguing that being but a limb of the dictator, the co-consul need not share his principal's fate. If anyone but Caesar were to die, his killing would be seen as an act of envy rather than a principled rejection of Caesar's "spirit" or way of tyranny. Indeed, Brutus, not disingenuously, wishes that there was some way to kill his spirit without shedding his blood. He fails to see that this way of killing Caesar will both poison his spirit and also spread it in the bloodiest way possible.

It seems also that Brutus, never having had a true friend, discounts the friendship and "ingrafted love" Mark Antony has for Caesar. So, he discounts Cassius' claim that the co-consul, being a "shrewd contriver" and having "means," could do much to thwart their success. Brutus feels that, loving Caesar so much, Antony could either die from grief or abandon himself to a life of dissipation, as one given to "sports, wildness and much company." The anti-social Stoic fails to see any potential for dangerous action in Caesar's virile and erotic friend. Brutus' idealism and Cassius' prudence are now very much at odds with each other; even as their plot threatens to tear the republic apart, there does not seem to be a plan in place for Rome's future after the assassination of Caesar. While Brutus looks to the past for legitimacy, Cassius seems resigned to seeking revenge only in the present. Grim anarchy looms ahead.

Brutus now receives another disturbing reminder of how alienated he is from himself when his cousin and wife, Cato's daughter (for at least this side of his lineage is not in doubt), comes to him with a sad remonstrance. Portia asks her husband why he forsakes her bed and refuses to take her into his confidence. This, the first external view we get of Brutus, suggests that he too, in his own way, is as mad or brutish in his behavior as Hamlet will appear. Portia represents the neglected and sleepless bodily aspect of Brutus. Though kind to his servant boy Lucio, Brutus is abrupt and dis-courteous towards Portia, his other (physical) self. While we noted earlier the probable reason for Brutus' inability to share the secret of his insecurity over his father's identity, this is no reason for him to not tell her of the plot against Caesar. After all, Cato the Younger was as renowned for his hostility to Caesar as his great-grandfather, Cato the Censor was towards Carthage. If the latter famously said *Carthago delenda est* at the end of each of his speeches, Cato the Younger just as relentlessly called for the destruction of Caesar and even committed suicide so as to deprive his enemy of the pleas-ure of sparing his life. After Junius Brutus, Cato the Younger was his nephew's other great role model. Indeed, Brutus could have also desired Caesar's death as revenge for this suicide.

But just as Brutus seems to be on the verge of confiding his thoughts and dark doubts to Portia, and perhaps even changing his mind, another miraculous pseudo-event pandering to his honor separates them. Ailing Ligarius appears, only to be miraculously healed by Brutus; this is taken as a sign that Rome will also be purified by him. If we follow the briskly paced events follow in *Julius Caesar*, Brutus and Portia will not meet again. Is she but deprived of a chance to play Andromache to his Hector? For better or worse, the fortunes of Brutus are now bound to those of his Cassius. It may also be noted that the influences of Cato and Cicero, Caesar's two greatest rivals, have been eliminated. We cannot but wonder what course events would have followed if Cicero and Portia had been consulted by Brutus. It is he who claims the power "to make sick men whole" even if it also makes "some whole sick." The first action could have been rigged by Cassius, but making the whole (of Caesar) sick will surely be the doing of Brutus and he. Yet it seems more likely that the whole to be made sick is Rome itself. The two friends fail to care for the common good.

Meanwhile the scenes with Portia, both with and without Brutus, reveal much about the quality of her love and the quantity of the noble Brutus' ability to love. While she offers ample proof of her ability to suffer silently for his sake through wounding herself grievously in the thigh, curiously the very place where Brutus will choose to stab Caesar, Brutus prefers healing Ligarius' false illness to caring for his wife's very real wound. He clearly values his intangible honor, and that of his perhaps mythical namesake and ancestor—whose reality he would prove along with his own legitimacy by killing Caesar—over his real wife's welfare. Portia, by comparison, after showing her ability to keep a secret that she does not know, almost reveals the secret after she infers what it is. That she does so reveals that her love for Brutus and care for his well-being exceeds the desire she has for revenge on Caesar for the death of Cato the Younger. But just as the beast meant to be sacrificed that day is found to be without a heart; Brutus, whose name means *dull* or *beast*, also seems heartless. Is his organ of love consumed by a mad lust for honor? Meanwhile Portia finally decides to let Brutus know she is merry, presumably signaling resigned support of his act. Following the action of the play (as we have noted), Portia and Brutus will never see each other again.

While this chapter is not about Caesar, he "as constant as the Northern Star" has self-certainty about who he is. In this he is most unlike Brutus, whose lack of self-knowledge is easily used by others, or even Cassius himself; the plotter uses manipulation as a means of denying his own envy and insecurity. At this point in his life Caesar is ultimately unafraid of rivals, omens, or events; as he has already attained recognition amounting to apotheosis, even kingship will only equate him to others. In his words, as quoted by Appian of Alexandria, "what need has he to be king, when he is already Caesar?" He seeks only to persist in that wondrous activity that makes him Caesar. Even his epilepsy is said to afflict him only in times of inactivity. But his erotic benevolence changes the nature of Rome; it makes men used to being powerful patrons into cringing clients, and discredits their anti-egalitarian way of living, and even its sacred basis. This is the true reason, the last *Senatus consultum ultimum* of Rome's *ancien regime* for his death.

He would also have to die in Rome in a way that would make him cease to be Caesar. Even his death abroad, and he would leave Rome in four days to campaign against Parthia in what was most likely his final campaign, would let him die as he had lived and thus consummate his apotheosis. Achilles, the psychopathic Phthian, perished before Troy to became an immortal memory, but Troy's conqueror and Greece's unifier, Agamemnon, met an ignominious death at home. This is why the faction had to act before Caesar left. Following this logic, Caesar had to be publicly killed and exposed as a tyrant in Rome. But this way of behavior would pit idealistic Brutus against crass Cassius. It would seem that the conspirators were not, or even could not be, decided how best to act after killing Caesar. This is almost inevitable since we know Brutus, their leader and public figurehead, to be deeply divided within, or more precisely, outside himself. Just as an Aristotelian tries to be a disembodied mind in a way that denies his soul and even philosophy, Brutus, trying to be a soul of honor, expels himself from his own soul and then from Rome itself. Denying the public good in the name of a ghostly ancestral Rome, he duly turns mad, melancholy and brutish. Only Antony, showing Caesar's clemency, and unwittingly repaying Brutus for earlier sparing his life, will save his honor.

Some sign of sleepless Brutus' anguish is shown when he arrives with the other conspirators to take Caesar to the Senate. When personally greeted by Caesar, who seems pleased at this early morning display of friendship, Brutus mutters in an aside that not all who seem Caesar's friends are truly like each other. He then goes on to say that this grieves his heart. Clearly none of the other notable Optimates gathered to kill Caesar share Brutus' deep qualms at what they are about to do. Brutus is meant by the Bard to appear as a Judas-like betrayer here. And even though Decius Brutus has played the important part of convincing Caesar to disregard all Calpurnia's prophetic fears and attend the Senate, only Marcus Brutus individually, severally and solitarily feels the conspirators' guilt. It could even be thought, as Brutus surely would have, that even his silent presence there may have made Caesar drop his guard. Mark Antony clearly implied as much when he told the shocked Roman mob that Brutus was Caesar's angel.

As Caesar and the faction approach Pompey's statue, Brutus seems to take control. He may have received Portia's message and been heartened by it. No ill augury has been drawn from Ligarius, whom he healed, not being with them. On the contrary while Cassius is suddenly all nerves and ready to kill himself, thus revealing the insecurity of an Epicurean in action, Brutus' Stoicism kicks in to make him constant. As Trebonius plays the vital task of diverting Antony, Brutus gives the order to surround Caesar and beg that an exile be forgiven. He needs to ritualize the ugly act ahead, to incorporate an account of a tyrant's slaying into the myths of rejuvenated Rome. It seems necessary that Caesar be provoked to speak with hubris; he does so, despising their groveling and comparing himself to the unmoved and constant Northern Star in a speech entirely of Shakespeare's making, before the Optimates kill him.

Caesar's last words are "*Et Tu, Brutè?* Then fall Caesar." The only Latin used in the play could be heard in many ways. We do not necessarily need to interpret them as Antony did, for rhetorical purposes to the mob. Said after Brutus has just stabbed him, in the groin we understand, the word *brute* also can mean "child" or "dull fool." Does Caesar mean something like, "You know not what you do"? Is Brutus addressed as a treacherous friend, as a fool, or as a child being reproached by his father? The ambiguity is left unresolved. It will haunt Brutus for the rest of his life. Was Caesar warning Brutus against the false friends with whom he had entered into the conspiracy? Or was he surprised that Brutus could not see that Caesar acted for the common good of Rome? Or that Brutus was his son? Just as Brutus struck him below the belt, Caesar could not have chosen words better suited to haunt his assassin.

But now Caesar lies dead and the conspirators must deal with the meaning of their deed. Unlike Casca and Cassius, who make grandiose proclamations to the people of liberty, freedom, enfranchisement, and the death of tyranny, Brutus seeks to quell the fears of the populace and tell them that "ambition's debt is paid." He seems to mean that Caesar was only guilty of desiring what Casca and Cassius accuse him of. He did yet not tyrannize the Romans, but had wished to, or perhaps had merely gained the power to do so. But again, even if Caesar's killers do not seem to agree why they did it, do they know what to do after this apocalyptic event? The first impulse of Casca and Brutus is to prepare for death, but Brutus then wishes to make their actions worthy of their deed. He proposes they bathe their arms and weapons in Caesar's blood before going to the Forum to proclaim "Peace, Freedom and Liberty" to the people. Cassius joins him in wishing to immortalize the universal and timeless significance of their tyrannicide. This is an updated version of the Lupercalia. Here too young aristocrats run through the city with weapons. The gruesome details of their deed are disguised by making it sacred theatre. Caesar is offered up to the gods. By this sacramental act, his murderers will be united as blood brothers and the moribund Republic will be rejuvenated.

It first seems likely that their act will be unopposed. The other consul, Antony, who earlier fled terrified, now sends word by a servant of his humble prostration to Brutus. Implying that he but feared Caesar but loves Brutus, and promising to love living Brutus more than dead Caesar, Antony shrewdly selects the weakest link in the conspiracy and homes in on his greatest vulnerability. Brutus is now bound by honor, vanity and guilt to behave in accord with the altruistic reasons he will offer for killing Caesar. Antony does not know them, but he knows Brutus better than Brutus knows himself. The rake will trick Brutus into doing his will. Cassius sees, but cannot warn Brutus against the very devices he had used on him. Cassius cynically made Brutus the figurehead of the conspiracy in order to make its intentions seem far better than they were; now Brutus acts as if all the killers of Caesar acted only from, and are forever bound by, the idealistic motives his weak ego gave his divided soul to justify joining the conspiracy. Prostrating himself as they did before Caesar, with the same murderous intent, Antony has just split up the faction.

There is much irony in Antony's pledge to "follow the fortunes of noble Brutus through the hazards of this untrod state with all true faith." As we see, he will follow "living Brutus" like a bloodhound since his true faith is to "dead Caesar." What happens when he "follows Brutus" to the rostrum at Caesar's funeral makes his words clear. But for now, Cassius must watch fearfully as Antony approaches Caesar's corpse; he wishes he would join them as a friend but his mind feels otherwise, and he warns Brutus that its suspicions are rarely wrong. We note that Antony never makes in person the pledges he made through his prostrated servant when he meets with Caesar's killers.

Once there, Antony artfully acts emotionally, thus letting Brutus, the self-professed Stoic, think himself superior and in control of the situation. "Living Brutus" carries himself as magnanimously as if he was (dead) Junius Brutus (or as proudly as Cicero after Cataline). But Junius Brutus, the idealized hero of seven centuries ago, is both less real and crueler than Brutus is, wants to, or can be. A perfect ideal of monumental history cannot sustain a man against the real blood fury, guilt and evil that poison his soul once he deliberately murders. This conflict is related to Hamlet and his father's furies, but Brutus' plight is worse as he is replacing an actual successful hero with a pre-historic myth that is false and corrosive. The idealized generosity he shows Antony is utterly inconsistent with the brutal way the faction murdered Caesar and the consul will use this to his advantage in his funeral oration. But he must first ensure there will be a funeral. By tradition a would-be tyrant's body could be dragged through the streets of Rome.

Even if such a deed was inconceivable, Antony flatters Brutus into trusting in his ability to persuade the mob of his honorable intentions. Brutus has also boasted that he will give excellent reasons why Caesar was dangerous; otherwise, as he himself concedes, his slaying would be no more than a spectacle. Revealing his ignorance of the deep ties binding father to son, Brutus then says, revealingly, "were you, Antony, Caesar's son you should be satisfied" by his sound reasons. Antony responds that he seeks naught else but a chance to speak as a friend at Caesar's funeral. The best occasion for Brutus to give his reasons would also be Caesar's funeral. Ergo, Caesar must have a funeral.

We can almost imagine Cassius' face here. As a good Epicurean, he knows that the ultimate particular carried far more power with the mob than airy ideas. Brutus is about to give the game away. He takes Brutus aside and tells him, almost echoing Caesar's last words, that he does not know what he does. Antony has the power to move the mob. Yet now the noble Brutus compounds his folly. Thinking his revived virtue and reason to be superior to the "gamester" Antony's crushed virility and rhetoric, Brutus will let him speak last at Caesar's funeral. He is convinced that, by speaking first and telling the crowd that Antony speaks by his permission, Caesar's ghost and the crowd will be satisfied. Although Cassius protests again, Brutus gives Caesar's body to Antony. His only condition is that Antony not blame them. He is otherwise free to speak all the good he can about Caesar and to say he does so by permission. It is only after Brutus leaves that Antony gives voice to his anger. He prophesies that a terrible fury will fall on Italy; Caesar's spirit will cry out for revenge and infernal strife will leave hell itself to wreak havoc. Passion is catching.

When Caesar's funeral occurs, we see Brutus and Cassius part company. While Brutus gives his oration, Cassius leaves to address another group of commoners elsewhere. We hear nothing further of this event or its result. Both funeral orations are Shakespeare's invention. Antony's is justly famous but Brutus' speech is just as remarkable for what it reveals about his divided and emotionally dishonest soul. He speaks to "Romans, countrymen and lovers" but his Rome is as abstract as the love he professes for it. Brutus' speech is all about himself and his honor: why *he* killed Caesar; the other conspirators and their respective motives are ignored, perhaps unintentionally. He asks to be believed for his honor and he asks the Romans to have respect for his honor that they may believe. The logic is as circular as Augustine's understanding seeking faith and faith seeking understanding; he lives in his ring of honor.

Brutus accuses Caesar of ambition and of trying to enslave Rome, but still cannot state the reasoning to support this charge in his own voice. He merely says, "the question of his death is enrolled in the Capitol." The Romans must trust his sacred honor. His speech seems to work, for the crowd is used to this pompous talk of Roman greatness, but the spell is broken when Antony takes the rostrum. By not directly accusing Brutus, he allows the mob to fill the gaps in his argument: Caesar's wounds. Still addressing Romans and countrymen, Antony substitutes "friends" for Brutus' "lovers." Friendship is a mutual relation between Antony and the Romans, and it is in this spirit that he comes down from the pulpit to join them, despite the risky time. By contrast, Brutus and the Romans are lovers of Rome, but not of each other. This love is as cold as the admiration Brutus has for Portia's pain. Antony says that Caesar's ambitions were for Rome's people, implicitly contrasting this to Brutus' self-centered and Stoic speech. Is this the "sterner stuff" ambition should be made of? Shouldn't love be more generous? It is in this spirit that he reveals Caesar's will to the Romans. Unlike Caesar's killers, who dipped their arms in his blood, Antony feeds the excited mob Caesar's raw flesh. This is pure Dionysian theatre. Antony has kept his word to Caesar, cried Havoc, and let slip the dogs of war. The murder is no longer abstract: Caesar's bloody body is exposed to the citizens and his spirit is reborn as fury.

Brutus' aside about Caesar's friends ("That every like is not the same") also reminds us of his last public words that none of his friends were untrue to him. Is this an indirect way of admitting that he betrayed many of his friends or is he saying that the betrayal of a friend causes the greatest pain of all? Is Brutus' enigmatic utterance completed by his last words, addressed to the furious ghost of Caesar, that he now kills himself far more whole-heartedly than he did when he administered that *coup de grace*? Does the guilt constantly felt after betray*ing* a friend exceed the pain felt at being betray*ed* by a friend? A betrayal leading to murder surely makes a culprit's experience of guilt all the more excruciating and unending. Brutus would play "scourge against scapegoat" but finds himself to be the true victim of his own evil. The sacred family "honor" he once valued so highly must seem false and ephemeral before the damage he did to his soul by giving into temptation. The pain from evil of this kind may be as undying as the soul itself. This tortured Hamlet; *pace* the Stoic consoling belief in suicide, we wonder if there is consciousness past physical death and if it is in our control? As his idealized Rome collapses, just as the false alliance between him and Cassius frays, Brutus' soul is unstrung and his guilty conscience makes Caesar's ghost appear from beneath his pseudo-Stoic façade to give the *coup de grace*.

Through Brutus and the conspiracy great and grievous damage was done to both Caesar and Rome. They could not think past Caesar's death but, as Antony saw, the evil Caesar did lived after him as Octavius. Caesar's angry ghost could not fix the harm done by the wars or restore Rome. His clemency and Eros died with Antony and Cleopatra. Following the loss of Caesar, its keystone—as constant as the Northern Star—Rome also breaks up, exploding like an unstable atom. Senators are murdered, civil war resumes, and the Republic tears itself apart. As many unstable alliances form and decay in a war between Rome and the Romans, even Brutus, the noblest Roman of them, falls apart. A tragic inconsistency between his name and words on the one hand and his needs and deeds on the other emerges. More than any other suicide, he literally dies of himself. We also find that there is no true friendship in this new unstable world; the deep myths holding the city together have been exposed. After Cassius' nominalism reveals

Caesar's mortality, Brutus' belief in the ideal of Rome is also revealed as hypocrisy by Antony. But, as self-knowledge depends on those we join with—whether friends or flatterers—Brutus and Cassius are corrupted by their alliance. So, even while Octavius and Antony infect each other with ambition and greed as they ruthlessly purge the Senate and loot the wealth of their proscribed victims, the two leaders of the plot against Caesar are seen to have gained each other's vices. Insecure Brutus is now manipulative and needy if not greedy, and blunt Cassius is ruled by empty Stoic rhetoric. Their original virtues are also compromised: Brutus' integrity is tarnished and Cassius' bold realism has turned fatalistic. It is against this backdrop that we rejoin them a year and a half since Caesar's murder. Their relation was not true friendship: it was not based on virtue or trust but was born of need close to desperation.

A Stoic moralist like Brutus needs an Epicurean to reveal ultimate particulars detached from Monistic necessity; yet when an Epicurean like Cassius is overwhelmed by passion and seduces a Stoic to hubris, both men lose their way. Brutus is now offended by Cassius' prudence; believing that he must be worthy of his deed as *the* slayer of Caesar, Brutus turns theatrical and hypocritical while hiding his violated integrity from the world. Having first wished to be worthy of his name, he is now bound to it. This disparity between name and soul makes Brutus the very "hollow man" he accuses Cassius of being when they finally meet up again. He even absurdly demands that Cassius levy money by the very means that he, Brutus, is ashamed of using. This shows Brutus to be just as manipulative as Cassius his seducer. Indeed, the whole quarrel scene between the two, taking place within Brutus' tent, can be seen as mainly occurring in Brutus' soul, with Cassius but witnessing an ugly scene of inner turmoil worthy of Hamlet himself. Even their quarrel has very much to do with Brutus' shame at being publicly chastised by Cassius, his erstwhile flatterer. Brutus, by virtue of his ancient name and noble nature, cannot be wrong even if the facts and logic do not support his pretensions; but we suspect that he also feels private anger for having been tempted and deceived by Cassius.

In this state Brutus will "outstare the lightning." Any imputation of wrongdoing or fallibility on his part will be seen as an offense against his ancestors and indeed Rome itself—the city they founded. Having killed Caesar, Brutus now is truly worthy of being called by this name and as such is also the very spirit of Rome. When Cassius at this juncture employs over-wrought rhetoric to bind himself to Brutus (who, in his overwrought state, all but demands love and flattery), Brutus in turn admits that he is, contrary to all his Stoic pretensions, deeply disturbed by his ignored wife's noble sui-cide. Once the two men first suspect and then see that their fortunes and friendship both follow a downward trajectory, they are much franker with each other. We will soon find that they already see suicide as the only hon-orable way out. Neither man expects to win nor knows how to rule were he to gain fortune's favor. In this context Stoicism and Epicureanism con-verge: the "ultimate particular" turns out to be a beautiful death. But while Cassius still hopes to fight a bit longer now that he's reconciled with Brutus, the figurehead of their cause, Brutus himself is too internally tormented by his guilt or madness to feel that he can maintain his Stoic façade any longer. This is why he is anxious to battle Antony and Octavius as soon as possible, even if it is to their best advantage to make the enemy come to them. Cas-sius the Epicurean, by contrast, does not suffer from these infernal interior qualms. He is as yet ruled by his intellect, even though the true direness of their situation is not hidden from him.

This abyss between Brutus' soul and Stoic façade also reflects the stark disparity between idealized Rome and the real city; ordinary Romans and Italians had to fight, suffer and be exploited to defend the Rome of Brutus and the Optimates. Brutus' lofty words conceal a gap only Caesar, as living *pontifex maximus*, could bridge. Caesar tried to exorcize Rome's ugly past and let Brutus display true virtue in a post-patriarchal city, but the scion of Junius could not accept the cost of being a free spirit. And even as his friend chides Brutus for not living in accord with his Stoic philosophy, Cassius' Epicureanism lurches towards fatalism as he continues to defer to Brutus' unhinged judgment. We see that neither is truly courageous for the sake of Rome or concerned with the common good of the Romans. While Brutus spends all of Act V being "absolute for death," mastery of Rome slips invis-ibly towards cold-blooded Octavius; this perfectly parallels the correspon-ding act in Hamlet where Young Fortinbras appears opportunistically to snap up a Danish Court that seems hypnotized by the spectacle of Hamlet's pyrrhic triumph over King Claudius.

But before Act V, and after his reconciliation with Cassius, Brutus must meet up with Caesar's ghost. This figure appears to be different from the ancestral spirits that seem to animate him—whether by their presence or absence. Julius Caesar is quite obviously not the same as Junius Brutus. And yet, in seeking confirmation that he is a worthy heir and bearer of the name of Brutus, and in doing so through actions that could surely have been occasioned by uncertainty about his legitimacy, Brutus has only succeeded in immortalizing the name of Caesar: the very man who may have fathered him. If his false consciousness has been of Julius, Brutus' deeds after Caesar's death have been ruled by Julius; we recall how his desperate desire to prove he had only the purest intentions in assassinating the dictator led to Antony's triumph at Caesar's pyre. In the famous words of Hamlet's mother, Brutus doth protest too much.

As noted before, Caesar's ghost's claim to be Brutus' "evil spirit" is consistent with Antony's claim that (only) "the evil men do lives after them" and his following assertion that Brutus was Caesar's "angel." While an angel is like a friend in being a good influence, helping a soul to see itself in the best light, this "evil spirit" tempted Brutus to see himself, wrongly, as the sole savior of Rome; it conceals from Brutus the pride, insecurity and jealousy that led him to deliver "the unkindest cut of all." Yet now, the ghost's terrifying presence and ominous words suggest (a) that it was wrong for Brutus to kill Caesar, and (b) that he became morally polluted and psychically blinded by this sin. We cannot forget that Brutus' behavior has already led to the death of his wife in a way that shamed him. This is only compounded by his blatant hypocrisy in playing the Stoic and pretending to be unaffected by the news of Portia's death. Brutus is now nothing more than a hollow man, filled with fear, shame and hypocrisy, but still serving as a figurehead for outdated Roman values that seem to be little better than their last embodiment. The Stoic virtue of his soul was extinguished symbolically by the death of Cato's daughter. Brutus' psyche is now encircled by his blind ancestral furies, his guilt towards Caesar, and Cassius' calculating cynicism. But, worse for his compromised cause, Brutus' stubborn selfishness seems doomed to help spread the monarchic ambition he sought to foil. But if he had reconciled with generous Antony, Caesar's best qualities might still have lived on—despite Octavius' reptile ambition.

Yet the ghost's appearance changes everything; it may be likened to how Dionysus being on stage in the *Bacchae* caused the death of tragedy. Here Brutus is forced to see that this "thing of darkness" exerted a powerful and toxic effect on his actions, standing between him and the self-knowledge he so desperately needs. This event is thus a moment of grace: Now that he has been shown what it is that has pervaded his mind and ruled his will, Brutus has a chance to tear himself apart from *his* "evil spirit" before going to Philippi. But is this truly a chance at redemption or an apocalyptic revelation of his own wicked soul that formally seals his doom? Even Cassius told Brutus, before tempting him, that his fault or fatal flaw is not in his star but in himself. Hamlet, we recall, had a similar epiphany when he met the gravedigger: Once he saw how life ends with bodily disintegration, there was no longer any need for him to be ruled by a dead king's evil spirit. Hamlet's reference to "imperious Caesar, dead and turned to clay" is apt: In *Julius Caesar* we seem to see Caesar not existing posthumously as himself but as a parasitic fury praying upon Brutus' bad conscience. But even as Hamlet was tempted to take on the needless duel with Laertes, Brutus was led to fight and die at Philippi by an inner mix of guilt, pride and fatalism along with contingent factors past anyone's control.

Even if Brutus came to Philippi half prepared to sue for peace, as his use of Antony's pregnant word "countrymen" hints, for surely as Romans they could have averted a bloodbath, Brutus would have had to abase himself before the triumvirs, risking life and losing dignity, but perhaps replacing Lepidus and healing Rome. He clearly lacked the prudent restraint Antony showed when he came before the assassins. When Antony, at this point, finally, brings up Brutus' murderous treachery towards Caesar, and the fawning flattery that the assassins showed their victim, he touches raw nerves and makes peace impossible. Cassius' angry words, reproaching Brutus for not killing Antony when they had the chance, and Octavius' drawn sword, cross the bridge between words and deeds. Now Brutus even indirectly accuses Antony of treason, and then says that it would be an honor for Octavius to die at his sword.

Yet when Brutus and Cassius rejoin their forces, they are not sanguine about their chances. Even if neither truly wishes to fight, their friendship is not of a kind that allows them be honest with each other. So, while Cassius, the sometime Epicurean, asks a friend to witness that he hazards his fortunes in one battle against his will, and talks of bad omens, Brutus—despite professions of Stoicism and criticisms of Cato's suicide—only admits to be too afraid of being paraded in a triumph to wish that fate simply prevail. Speaking in the third person, he claims that "Brutus" would never "go bound to Rome" for "He bears too great a mind." His public persona is too ruled by its name for him to speak or act otherwise. The Optimates take leave of each other admitting ignorance of what lies ahead but hoping against hope to meet again: "This same day must end that work the Ides of March began." So, while the evil they have done lives long after them, their best intentions now have little hope of survival. If the two killers have not shared virtues, they have exchanged vices: while Brutus' hesitant care for honor and Stoic fatalism have infected his blunt brother-in-law, Cassius' manipulative ways are now used by Junius Brutus' once-scrupulous scion.

While Brutus and Cassius never meet again, their failure to see, trust or communicate adequately with each other has much to do with their deaths. While Brutus meets with initial good fortune against Octavius, his mad wish to end the battle and be resolved with Caesar's ghost surely influenced his desire to over-pursue the fleeing foe as much as his inexperience. We may also infer that Brutus' underpaid forces were more inclined to break ranks and loot, instead of defeating Octavius. Meanwhile Cassius, his men depleted by desertion and encircled by Antony, retreats and sends Titinius, his "best friend," on his own horse, like Patroclus, to scout the identity of an advancing force. But now Cassius, whose "sight was ever thick," is afflicted with the inability to tell friend from foe that he had previously exploited in Brutus. Concluding falsely that by using Titinius as a decoy, he betrayed his friend to the enemy and feeling shame at this act of a "coward," Cassius commits suicide—using the very sword that stabbed Caesar. We see his Epicurean grip on the ultimate particular only extend to bad things; ruled by his envy, fear and pride, Cassius shrewdly sucks evil from a human ego, but cannot see goodness in a soul, an event, or the cosmos.

As Messala realizes, Cassius suffers from "mistrust of success ... hateful error, melancholy's child." He poignantly asks personified error why it "shows to the apt thoughts of man, the things that are not?" Thus, thick-sighted Cassius sees only Caesar's flaws, never his greatness. The contrary of idealism, which believes in good things that could never be, this cynicism sees evil motives where they do not exist. A terrible moral malaise that persists to the present day, this mistrust of error believes in sin and vice; this perverse theology also makes it possible for misanthropic moralists to profit from punishing the imagined vices of their victims. While this outlook also explains Cassius' "itching palm," the basis of the master conspirator's cynical wisdom is revealed as disguised cowardice. This pusillanimity explains his deference to moralistic Brutus, who seems to never fear doing what's right. We also grasp the righteous Roman way of growing rich fighting "defensive wars" and punishing the perceived vices of others.

Returning too late, finding Cassius dead, Titinius will commit suicide after Messala leaves to bear the sad news to Brutus. He believes that, like Cassius' slave, Pindarus, who earned emancipation by slaying his master, all Rome too will now be cast into freedom and chaos. But, like the plebians, Messala will be far more pragmatic in his choice of masters; first transferring his allegiance from Cassius to Brutus, he will then follow Antony's fortunes before finally abandoning him for Octavian. Titinius and Messala seem to represent the tragic and comic options available to all followers; a wise man can either die nobly or live long and profitably in the shadow of another's success. As we may now see, even Brutus has devoted his life to the second option. He lives through, with, and in his mythic ancestor.

Now Brutus comes with Young Cato, his other brother-in-law. Owning that Caesar rules, even in death ("mighty yet, thy spirit walks abroad and turns our swords in our own proper entrails"), he calls the two dead men "the last of all the Romans," making explicit what Messala implied: Rome itself ceased to be with Cassius' death. But Brutus cannot even honor Cassius as he once allowed Antony to praise Caesar, spiriting the corpse away for fear that the sight of it would dishearten his men. As with Portia, he cannot voice—or even know—his true sense of loss and pain. Brutus does not own his soul or rule his passions; aware only of his noble name and airy ideals, he lived in a mythic past and idealized future, not in the present. While *Julius Caesar* shows how superstitious the Romans were towards external events, Brutus only seemed to feel interior/psychic forces. Just like a woman whose whole world is her children, or an autistic denizen of our techno-tribal world, Brutus was blind to other human souls and indifferent to external objective realities. He tried to view Rome through the eyes of his ancestors but ended up seeing Caesar's ghost. His vision was apocalyptic; it revealed the true object of his unconscious passion to be Julius Caesar, not Junius Brutus.

Brutus is now a silent brute. As Aristotle once said, and as Caesar's dying words seemed to echo, a man is a brute without a city. Cato and Brutus are now overtly what they have always been: mere walking shadows of their illustrious ancestors. In a very real sense Brutus can no longer know himself; without Rome and Cassius he is as self-forsaken as deposed Richard II. He cannot function as a free man. Life to him is meaningless without Rome. And his conscience is as polluted by Caesar's murder as his civic consciousness is blinded by Cassius' death. They call each other "countrymen" but will no longer say "Rome" or "Roman." They have no city and their country is a wasteland. Octavius will soon claim to begin an age of peace, but these men now suffer the truth about Rome. To quote Tacitus: "They made a desert and call it peace." Yet, as Young Cato and Brutus try to free their outlawed souls, to escape living death by dying with honor, other alienated men impersonate them and seek glory by decoying their foes.

After Brutus leaves, urging his "countrymen," "O, yet hold up your heads," Young Cato shouts in response to him, "what bastard will not?" His words prefigure the replacement of the Republic by family in the age of empire, but also remind us that Brutus may link himself with Rome to disguise the murky circumstances of his own birth. With the fall of the Rome of the fathers, they now all seem illegitimate and this putative bastardy is best refuted by dying for the city. But even if Lucilius and Young Cato seem slightly comic in seeking to die as Brutus and Marcus Cato, we see magnanimity, however misplaced, in their conduct. While Young Cato vindicated his father by dying in battle, Lucilius tried to die as Brutus to make it easier for him to flee Philippi and rally his faculties and forces. If he were to escape, their reputations might at least be salvaged for posterity. His disgrace will surely seal their doom.

Yet Antony, ever responsive to loyalty, shows him that virtue and friendship can be rewarded beyond the range of partisan politics and the patriarchal city; ordering that Lucilius be "given all kindness," he proclaims that he "would rather have such men my friends than enemies." If the city or something better is to be rebuilt, its foundation must be friendship. This is echoed, implicitly, when we next find Brutus in *Julius Caesar's* last scene. By having him say "Come poor remains of friends, rest on this rock," Shakespeare could be subtly implying that patriarchal Rome and the Petrine

Roman Church are somehow linked through the death of Caesar and opposition to his anti-elitist political program. Even as Brutus and Cassius betrayed their followers while they fought for the Senate and an oppressive patriarchal oligarchy, and despite his reputation as a "masker and reveler," the very traits that led many to see Caesar's erotic clemency with disdain, Antony stuck to Caesar's cause and practiced the rare power to unmask, reveal and reward virtue in any man. The plot of *Julius Caesar* suggests that Antony can offer Brutus' men what they falsely believed their leader to have. But though he won the Battle of Philippi, Antony was tied by fate to Octavius, a man who chased infinite ambitions with Brutus' priggish hypocrisy and Cassius' calculating cowardice. So, Caesar's dreams would die again.

Defeated in battle by Mark Antony, and his last scout, Statilius, having been either captured or killed, Brutus is now bereft of hope. Claiming that it is better to leap in to the pit than to be pushed in, he asks his old schoolmate to kill him. When Volumnius declines on the ground that this office could not be done by a friend, Brutus makes his final speech. As mentioned earlier, he tells his last "countryman" of "his" joy that "in all my life, I found no man but he was true to me." While his refusal to use the words "friend" or "Roman" is striking, effectively denying the Roman-ity or friendship of his last faithful followers, Brutus' sad words also seem to accept that he was not cheated by anyone, granting that he hurt himself and died by his own hands for his own sins. The fault is not in our stars.

The tragic spectacle of Brutus' death grieves Antony who, calling Brutus "the noblest Roman of them all," generously says that he alone of the Optimate conspirators was recruited by thought of the common good. It leads us to believe that Antony would have been willing to extend Caesar-like clemency to Brutus, similar to that which Caesar once gave Cassius and Brutus, and Octavius showed Ovid's future patron: Messala. It would have been so much to Antony's advantage if Brutus had been beside him to resist Octavius' ambitions and protect Rome itself.

Even if its historic likelihood is but a Shakespearean conceit, there is a lesson to be had from his thought exercise. If Brutus had accepted his Caesarean rebirth via Antony's clemency, Julius Caesar's legacy would have been vastly different. Antony, Octavius and Brutus, Caesar's three favorites, would have ruled Rome as they were supposed to in his absence during the long Parthian campaign. While Antony, as his role at the Lupercalia shows, would have embodied Caesar's erotic virility (and married Calpurnia), Brutus would have resumed his place as Caesar's moral compass or angel; joined with ambitious but intelligent Octavius, Caesar's legal heir, they would form a triumvirate that might have rejuvenated the sick Republic. Each man could have served as a check on the other two triumvir's shortcomings, provided each other with much needed self-knowledge, and advanced the common good. This outcome could have been Caesar's truest and best legacy to Rome. Instead, his erotic virtues were buried with his bones while Caesar's furies lived after him in Brutus, Octavius and Antony; instead of working together as friends, Romans and countrymen, these three extraordinary men only succeeded in bringing out the worst in each other.

When Strato says, "Brutus only overcame himself," Lucilius welcomes this proof of his prediction: "no enemy shall ever take alive the noble Brutus … he will be found like Brutus, like himself." He prayed "gods defend him from so great a shame." But that being taken alive is seen as "shame" is more significant. Does Brutus' honor prevent him from being captured or escaping punishment? Before their final parting, both Cassius and Brutus infected each other with new and unwelcome self-knowledge: while Cassius finally felt shame in being exposed as a coward, Brutus came to see that, like Marcus Cato, he was as afraid of receiving clemency from his base enemies as he was of being paraded through Rome's streets in triumph. But is inner guilt or public shaming what he tries to escape by his suicide? And are the two mutually exclusive? Like Hamlet, he has an interiority of soul (thus he calls Cassius "hollow"), which none of *Julius Caesar*'s other characters has or imagines him to own. With Brutus the focus in Shakespeare's drama moves from a world ruled by God or gods to darker forces working within and beneath the individual moral agent. Like Hamlet, Brutus has bad dreams. He suffers from what Dostoevsky would later call a surplus of consciousness. Perhaps this is why thumotic self-identity in death seems to mean far more to him than the erotic vulnerability of a life extended by Antony's clemency. Indeed, clemency itself is a Caesarean virtue that as such is doubly unwelcome. In receiving it, Brutus would indirectly owe his life to Caesar and thus accept Caesar's ghost as his father. In doing so he would indirectly sully his mother's chastity and even sacrifice his very right to bear the old honorable name of Brutus.

The tragedy of Brutus is that *pace* Lucilius he was hardly ever Brutus. Despite the warning from the ghost, he had to go to Philippi; his sense of ancestral honor was stronger than mind or conscience. It was the desire to emulate his father that made Hamlet fight his fatal duel with Laertes. Rome's respect for his name ruled his self-image but the Romans did not know this or he them. They neither fathomed his depths nor felt his true shallowness. Perhaps Brutus was even a mystery to Caesar, a man so confident in his identity that he spoke in the third person of himself without irony. Readers of *Julius Caesar* must not fall into Cassius' plot (Hamlet's "Mousetrap") and let Shakespeare's mischievous stagecraft tempt us into admiring Brutus, its disastrous unreliable protagonist; we must not be tricked to believe that we see the action of the play as they did, through their eyes. The Bard plays this game with us with Richard III and Henry V, but it is by comparing Brutus to Richard II that we see how this complex character evolved.

The tension in Brutus between name and soul may be likened to that between Richard as king and man. Both seemed to live in words rather than deeds for a while, and their entry into the real world is as short and bad for them as it is awful for their people. Richard's view of himself as God's deputy parallels Brutus' pontifications about his great mind and pretended Stoic *apatheia*. Both have noble and loving wives whom they neglect: in Richard's case homoerotic activity is implied, while Portia's self-inflected thigh wound is a sign that she was sexually ignored. The two men put so much energy into playing these roles that they lost self-knowledge. In all these respects, they prepare the English stage for Hamlet. Brutus is so obsessed with his ancestral honor that he cannot, for all his talk of the general good, equate it with what Antony calls the "common good." What's good for "his" Rome is good for the commoners, not *vice versa*. His Rome is a regime he has inherited and must hand on; making plebs his equal violates the rights of the dead. Brutus holds his honor in common with them. Even if he were open to Caesar creating a more egalitarian order, he has no right to speak for his patrician ancestors, changeless in their wisdom and virtue. A radical change to Rome's eternal essence delegitimizes the Optimates and dishonors their ancestors.

Caesar's greatness, like Napoleon's, was gained by recognizing the humanity of the many and devoting his life to fighting those entitled few who found glory in each other's eyes by holding the *demos* down, though he was certainly not beyond deriving power, riches and erotic satisfaction in doing so. But Brutus, Cassius and their peers saw glory in zero-sum terms. They shared in their ancestors' glory by defending the line dividing the few from the mob; it is this collective consciousness, even if it is usually felt by some as guilt or a burden, that Brutus (or Hamlet) cannot be freed from. A Brutus would rather be despised by his ancestors (and admired by those lesser beings whom he duly despises in turn) than see a brave new world, as redeemed by a Caesar or Christ, through the eyes of a free spirit. Even as these men have sleepless nights and fear bad dreams, they prefer not to control their own consciousness. When Eumaeus told Odysseus that the gods take away half of a man's wits when he becomes a slave, he was too slavish to admit that, far from being forcibly deprived of freedom of thought, the enslaved men often surrender what Dostoevsky called their "surplus of consciousness" all too willingly; a secure life as a slave within a stable but artificial city or economy is often preferred over being an outlaw or free spirit in the ugly chaos outside city walls. We cannot imagine what it is to be unprotected by civilization's cosmopolitan categories. This is why the *Odyssey*'s beggars usually told lies and slaves only testified under torture. Aristotle, the father of logic, did not see that a man without a city might be a thing other than a beast or god. He may also be sleepless and mad. It is difficult for us to see naked reality *tout court* without socially built intervening categories to protect our minds.

I believe that what's left suggestively unexplained in *Hamlet* can be known by looking to Brutus and vice versa. The parallels between their two plays suggest Brutus is as mad as Hamlet. Neither apologizes for the mad categories or rules that define his actions. While the one is literally a beast or brute without a city, a hamlet is a town without a church. Brutus is ultimately brutalized by his very name. His unholy attachment to it makes him a brute incapable of friendship or civic life and ultimately brings down Rome—the city he loves so much. Both men are key figures of a failed transition from corrupt old regimes to brutal empires; the evil of their deeds outlasted the good intentions they piously professed in speech. Even if Shakespeare's fears of a militant European empire, a nightmare almost realized by Philip II, Cromwell or Gustavus Adolphus and embodied in *Hamlet* by Fortinbras, never came to pass, his hope that a Classical or Christian humanism could emerge from the chaos of the Reformation was never to be.

This tragedy is titled "*Julius Caesar,*" not "Brutus," since Octavius never fulfils Caesar's populist plans but becomes the true heir of Cassius and Brutus. As we recall, a poet tried to reconcile the two when they quarreled. Is this not Virgil? How is it that, 1600 years later, Hamlet never looks to the public good and neither do his eulogists? Or that this Roman-Lutheran prince proscribes friends and drives his beloved to suicide without critical protest? He but follows Brutus, Octavius and Virgil. Put simply, both Caesar and Jesus inspired political and theological emancipatory events that Octavius' empire and Constantine's church limited and used as a basis for literary/moral authority. Worse, the mindless, repressive and hierarchical tradition based on the fusion of these two powers was retroactively falsified, purified, and made sacred. It is not tragic but bitterly ironic that Henry V, God's anointed scourge and Augustinian avenger of evil, is seen today as a model Christian king. Yet in *Julius Caesar* the Bard exposes the origins of an anti-egalitarian tradition that used Caesar's name (not Brutus') in vain to end the Republic and build an empire; it then reversed Jesus' moral revolt by making Christianity an enslaving, scapegoating, imperial faith. Shakespeare would help late Elizabethan England find a *via media* between a corrupt old faith and its savage new offshoots; we see that neither Caesar's murder nor Jesus' crucifixion redeems man from evil or serves the common good. Neither must we trust in our own arms to be free, as Machiavelli urged; we pray instead to see all souls with rich eyes and empty hands.

CHAPTER FOUR
KING LEAR AND THE DEATH OF GOD

Since an original reading of *King Lear* will serve as the cornerstone of this book, functioning both as the text confirming our interpretation of *Hamlet*, and the performance revealing the most substantial account yet of Shakespeare's suggested reform of Christianity, it seems best to approach this play directly. By refusing to let *King Lear* be framed by any prior assumptions about how it must be read, and by permitting neither King Lear nor King James to demand that we approach this text in a certain way, we allow what is both obscene and sublime about *King Lear* to emerge. As with the *Bacchae*, which all but terminated the genre of tragedy by allowing the god Dionysus to appear without Apollonian mediation, the Bard's many deep and subtle reflections on the nature of authority and rule reach their apocalyptic culmination in his revelation of the mad old king, stripped of all power and protection, being humiliated by nature as he crawls towards death. Shakespeare has already proved his mastery of the art of dark magic, his unmatched power to seduce us into seeing a play through the eyes of a villain; this is why we must watch both *King Lear and ourselves* very closely as the Bard stages what may well be his greatest tragedy. None of the lines a character speaks, however eloquent, should necessarily be thought to represent a true state of affairs; they could also stem from deceptive intent or self-deception.

This means that just as the aging king of Britain prepares to dispossess himself of all his power and possessions, we too should take equal care to view him in this diminished light; Lear is no longer the sacred figure he once was. He might claim in his madness to be every inch a king, but he is not; he will have succeeded in accomplishing what Duke Vincentio, in *Measure for Measure* tried, albeit disingenuously, to do. Lear's self-brewed storm will soon wash the sacred balm off his anointed brow. But, if this is possible, can it be that other sacred bonds can also be dissolved? Not long before Shakespeare's birth, another king used his sovereignty to divorce himself from both his Spanish queen and his Roman pontiff. But if this is possible, if nothing is sacred, can a man sever the ties binding him to a king? Also, if the sacred itself is defunct, is there a god? We will find that *King Lear* tacitly probes the dizzying implications of these many challenging questions. No longer will it be feasible for man to remain innocently unaware of the power of the logos/word.

Despite the casual reader's common belief, Lear's dramatic act of abdication does not occur *ex nihilo*. *King Lear's* opening words are spoken by two old courtiers, Kent and Gloucester; they discuss the relative standing of the two royal sons-in-law, the Dukes of Albany and Cornwall, in a way which suggests that there is something rotten in the house of Lear. But this state of tension between the dukes, literally the warlords protecting the North and South of the kingdom, also implies that they themselves are jockeying for position and destabilizing the very land they are supposed to defend. Indeed, since France and Burgundy are suitors for Cordelia's hand, it may even seem that these foreign potentates are needed to save the kingdom from its guardians. As for the two old earls—representatives of England proper by their titular counties—their part is only to obey but not minister to a king. Lear's acts are ruled by "affections" rather than reasons.

This implied mastery of volitional over moral considerations is repeated when the subplot of *King Lear* is introduced. We find that Gloucester has an illegitimate son: Edmund. His bastard follows him to Lear's court and will be silently present when the king makes his formal test of love before renouncing the throne. Before this, he will hear his sire speak cavalierly about the "good sport" that led to his conception. Gloucester will then tell Kent that after having been "out" for nine years, Edmund shall now be sent "away" again. No reasons are given for these unnatural and long separations. Despite its moral inhumanity, old Gloucester's treatment of his illegitimate son is perfectly lawful; this anticipates Lear's arbitrary behavior towards his children. The law sustains the willful rule of old men over their offspring. And yet, even if nothing can presently militate against it, it is from this very nothing that the come-uppance of the patriarchs will soon emerge. In short, if a few rich old men claim that their wanton wills and words give them power over everything, it is out of all that has no right, status or existence in their artificial world that true justice slowly comes. The illegitimacy of the natural cannot be proclaimed by the rich and powerful for too long with impunity. *King Lear* and Euripides' *Bacchae* both teach the same tragic lesson to the proud. Absolute monarchs who proclaim that "error has no rights" suffer from a hubris that blinds all who posit it; this leads them to commit massive acts of moral excess that cannot be ignored. Sins performed on this grand scale necessarily engender cosmic retribution.

It is not the socially invisible Edmund but Gloucester who is sent away before Lear administers his love test. As was the case in *King John,* only the Bastard is present to witness acts of state with far-reaching implications being performed by his betters for manifestly private and personal reasons. It is for "Commodity" or convenience that Lear will miraculously turn one into three; he will have the gall to tear the spiritual substance of England into three unstable parts so that partially wielded power is transubstantiated into love. Yet both bastards are partially blind: while *King John*'s bastard cannot see for a while that John's surrender of his empire *willy-nilly* restores England's integrity—unlike Lear who tears it apart—*King Lear*'s Edmund only sees an opportunity to advance himself and gain revenge on both his father and half-brother. It is also striking that just like Edmund who has been "out nine years," *King John* and *King Lear* are nine years apart. This is a strong hint that we should view the action of the opening scene of *King Lear* through the eyes of one like Edmund, a child victimized by a partial and irresponsible parent; Lear's giving up of all his power and land must be completed by stripping away the respect and sanctity others may think him to possess inherently. A prodigal father may not expect to find himself loved equally by his angry children.

This is why Shakespeare's re-telling of the older story of Leir and his daughters is distinctively changed by the addition of the subplot featuring Edmund; it is not merely the metaphysical scale of Lear's rage at Cordelia's silence that makes *King Lear* sublime—we also have added reason for the seemingly callous conduct of the two older daughters. Both Goneril and Regan seem to have been exposed to the same arbitrary lack of favor from their father that Edmund received from Gloucester. This is why, denied love, all three of them find it natural to employ deceit and flattery to gain power from and then mistreat a father who never showed them true affection. Goneril and Regan must also deceive Lear if they love their spouses— so as to add to their lands. We must recognize that most family talk, like family values, lives in an atmosphere of platitudes.

When Lear announces his "darker purpose" to divide "our kingdom," he suggests that he does so in part to prevent "future strife" between his two "sons," Albany and Cornwall, who are married to Goneril and Regan. Equating "nature" with "merit," and measuring worthiness by rhetoric, he bids his daughters to earn larger shares of his kingdom by making the fullest profession of love for him. While Lear is not expecting sincerity, their coerced pledges have performative impact and binding power. But since their words only express personal affection to him rather than loyalty to England itself, this ceremony, like John's second coronation in *King John*, will at best only focus attention on Lear as the divided land's spiritual leader—even after his abdication.

When Goneril and Regan duly comply with Lear's wish, the one situating her feelings beyond the very limits of language and the other declaring her hostility to anything other than concern with Lear's happiness, Cordelia refuses to play the game any further by announcing that she can say nothing that would outbid her sisters and win the greatest share of Lear's realm. Though both her sisters have also said nothing, albeit in more ambiguous terms, with Goneril taking refuge in the ineffable and Regan not saying if her exclusive concern with Lear's happiness is benign or malign, Cordelia's impolitic bluntness deeply offends her father. Her excuse that she must reserve half her love, care and duty for her future spouse angers him even more. Also, Cordelia may not wish to outbid her sisters; taking lands designated for them would only sow seeds for future discord. As the only one who may have seen the map before, she would not wish this.

Lear proceeds to disown Cordelia, effectively delegitimizing his favorite daughter and making her a stranger to his heart and himself forever. She has dashed his plans to set his "rest on her kind nursery." For this sin Cordelia is exiled forever from his sight. It seems as if he expected Cordelia to renounce any claim to "the vines of France and the milk of Burgundy" for his sake. She would then don the un-conferred coronet on display as his regent and queen. Any threat to England would be checked by France and Burgundy both hoping to wed Cordelia after Lear dies. That's how *King Leir* originally ends—Cordelia returns to rescue Lear, defeat her sisters and rule England for many years. But our Bard, more perverse than Cordelia, had very different ideas.

Though choosing "truth" over the "tenderness" Lear all but demanded of her, and refusing the cynical relativism Lear and her two older sisters adhere to, Cordelia is yet unable to articulate this "truth" in words. Even her appeal that Lear confirm her fault was "tardiness in nature" or a reticent tongue will not reveal the true reasons for their sudden estrangement. It seems that one cannot reason with Lear; the only options he offers are flattery and acquiescent silence. As in a comedy, the only way out is by retreat to nature and reversing a stubborn father's will. But in *King Lear,* paradoxically but fittingly, it is the angry father, Lear himself, who enters the state of nature and learns to speak honestly. In his patriarchal state sincerity is forbidden, even for him.

The circumstances leading to Kent's equally abrupt banishment further support this view. After first warning the old earl not to intervene when he disclaims Cordelia, "come not between the dragon and his wrath," Lear explodes again when his loyal servant unrelentingly tells him off. Addressing his king as a man by using the familiar "Thou," Kent doggedly accuses Lear of folly, madness, rashness, bowing to flattery, and of doing evil; he does not desist even when the maddened king draws his sword to kill him. Kent claimed to have been the "true blank," i.e. the target or objective conscience of his king; his life itself was but a pawn that he'd gladly sacrifice to thwart his monarch's enemies. While, as we shall see, he will faithfully match his deeds to his words, even after being exiled, it yet remains to be seen if Lear deserves such absolute loyalty.

Lear's furious accusation, "thou hast sought to make us break our vows" makes little sense since he has not sworn by anyone other than himself. The king's loud oaths by "the sacred radiance of the sun, the mysteries of Hecate and the night," or even "the operations of the orbs by whom we exist and cease to be" is bombast; having banished his heart and eyes—Kent and Cordelia—from himself, Lear is now little more than empty words draped over an old, naked, and ugly will. But who or what then was Lear truly? And how did he seem to command the absolute fidelity of both Cordelia and Kent until, and even beyond, this ultimate act of senile willfulness?

Lear's behavior is especially striking in that he holds himself answerable to no higher power; he acts as if by divine right and *King Lear* strongly suggests that he bears an allegorical resemblance to the Post-Reformation God in whose name monarchs made claim to absolute power. According to such an interpretation, while Goneril and Regan could readily be likened to the Catholics and Calvinists in their fulsome praise language, which necessarily overshot the limits of reason and logos, Cordelia must be more like the Elizabethan Church in its tenuous and short-lived attempt to steer a *via media* between the other two extreme stances. Indeed, to the extent that such a prudent position would strictly follow the Mosaic commandment not to use the divine name in vain, silent Cordelia may also even seem to emulate the first "chosen people" of God, the Jews, in their original favor and later displacement and persecution by two newer and more populous monotheistic faiths: Christianity and Islam. This parallel also holds up if we contrast the fervent Protestantism and militant Catholicism of Edward VI and Mary to Elizabeth's windowless soul. But by James I's time, things had reached a point where philosophy and even theology had to render new justifications of the willful ways of gods and kings to angry bare forked men. If the Reformation began with Martin Luther's terror in a thunderstorm, its truest implications would only be revealed by an imagined but equally apocalyptic storm created by William Shakespeare.

Lear's demand for unconditional, exclusive and limitless praise and love was denied by Cordelia on the credible grounds that this would make it impossible for her to love her husband. But we could also extend this limit heavenward; Lear wishes to be praised as if he is the jealous deity of Moses. This is why, when checked or curbed by his older daughters, he will then threaten to break God's promise to Noah and destroy everything in a dreadful storm of his own brewing. In *King John* we saw John and the Bastard stand up to hubristic papal absolutism in a way that brought England into existence. But this is also why all claims to absolute kingship by divine right must be rejected. Now, in a play set in England's primal past, we see Lear divide this very land up just so he may enjoy quasi-divine retirement from the obligations of kingship. But *King Lear* helps us see that he is not only denying the spiritual integrity of both soul and country by laying claim to divine right: Lear is inadvertently revealing that even God should not be conceived of in this absurd way. The God revealed by Jesus is the transcendent source of all love; as such, he would not deny or make illegitimate all kinds of love that are not solely dedicated to him. But this is not Lear's way; just like kings of Shakespeare's time, who derived their legitimacy from Paul's sycophantic claim that all power is from God, the old king seeks divine authority and demands unconditional love even as he relinquishes political power and denies any responsibility for evil.

Edmund, the antihero of this play, will have *King Lear*'s scapegoat Cordelia treated as Arthur was in *King John*; they were both too pure to wield power effectively in their sordid world. This is why, like *King John*'s Bastard, who embraced gain as his lord on seeing that commodity was the "bias of the world," Edmund proclaims Nature as his goddess. Left unnoticed on the stage while Lear divides his kingdom and banishes Cordelia and Kent, Gloucester's natural son just may have heard Goneril and Regan finally speak the ugly truth about the once sacred person of their father. Now they have successfully flattered their way out of his overbearing sway, the two sisters find common cause in planning to address their father's increasingly chaotic and willful ways. Noting that he has "ever but slenderly known himself" and has always behaved rashly, they have reason to fear that Lear's behavior will only "worsen with the waywardness ... infirm and choleric years bring." While their words sound unfilial and ungrateful, we cannot forget that these two unfavored sisters have probably suffered neglect and unfair treatment at Lear's hands. Like Edmund, they will take revenge on those who caused or benefitted from their long years of humiliation.

We cannot doubt that Edmund will have gained "much matter" from seeing Lear's self-indulgent performance at his abdication. The embrace of Nature and pledge to serve her law only comes naturally from Edmund's repudiation of the "plague of custom" that has not only treated him unfairly but also allows men like Lear to act with ill-mannered petulance to those who are bound by the same contagious customs to indulge his every mad whim. Vowing to no longer be ruled by "curiosity of nations," technicality of law, or anything that would falsely distinguish between his brother and himself, merely because Edgar was not born of love but from a "dull, stale, tired bed," and crying, "Now gods, stand up for bastards," Edmund sets out to legitimize himself. But forging crooked letters with a fair hand leads only to the denial of there being any truth at all.

Nominalism, if not nihilism, results naturally from men seeing that old customs, far from serving the common good, are only used to justify selfishness and vice. When their victims see that there is no true difference in kind between the arbitrary actions of an autocrat and the chaos caused by a criminal, they conclude that only real distinction is between skill and ineptness in the use of political power. In contrast to Lear and Cordelia, who failed to play the game of thrones with Machiavellian *virtù*, Goneril,

Regan and Edmund set out to gain glory and power for themselves. But can these self-assertive values repair the moral chaos Lear has created?

By splitting his realm to suit his personal convenience, Lear placed England in grave jeopardy. Old Gloucester's words, "Kent banished thus, and France in choler parted," hint that Lear's final parting with the French king, without Kent to advise him, has made the divided nation's plight even more perilous. The earl's failure to mention Cordelia's exile is also striking but it must be passed over now. Our first focus must be on Edmund and his revenge on Gloucester and Edgar.

Gloucester is from Tolstoy's world; he is unaware that he has sired a Trotsky. Edmund's creative use of literacy against his brother reveals to us that Gloucester, like so many sufferers from rich old male entitlement (ROME), is ontologically blind. It is absurd to view mere senility as sublime wisdom, or to hold what is selfish or sentimental to be sacred. Ruled by the "plague of custom," which forbids them the skeptical scrutiny of an individual soul, a sanctified habit or an ancient institution, men are infected by folly and lose respect for their best powers of heart and mind.

Edmund's deception of Gloucester and Edgar is so ridiculously easy that we must conclude that what takes place is compressed and symbolic rather than a realistic representation of an event. He uses fake news to demonstrate the timeless truth of how readily ignorant men are led by written or reported words to discount all they know of someone close to them. While in old Gloucester's case this susceptibility is perhaps compounded by a guilty awareness of having been negligent in caring for his sons, Edmund—rationalist and follower of Nature—will surely include both religion and morality on the list of things he is liberated from. As Edmund's letter puts it, he will no longer accept "the idle and fond bondage in the oppression of aged tyranny." Credulous respect for old men and older forgeries should not curb free spirits from passing up on the chance of writing new and equally persuasive charters that give power to men who can exercise it best. If Gloucester depends on Edmund to assure him that the writing on the letter was Edgar's, this need makes the lettered illegitimate son his foolish sire's better. All Gloucester does is find bad astrological reasons for what Edmund's rhetoric has already convinced him of.

Edgar meanwhile is too noble to doubt Edmund's word that their father is ill-disposed towards him; perhaps, since he seems to be one of Lear's hundred knights, he is used to the mercurial ways of old men. But, nevertheless, his deference towards his elders leads him to humor and defer rather than to ask cause and speak reasonably with his father. Again, it seems that laws exist for the prerogatives and powers of the older instead of defending the natural rights of the young. It is in this unfair context that Edmund, deprived of lands by birth, will gain power by his wit; he is well content to be in a place where he may use others' folly to shape his own destiny. Lear had ruled by commanding men; Edmund hopes to succeed by manipulating human vices. But his opportunism spawns great dangers, moral and political, in a state where all souls buckle under pressure; corruption pervades a realm where neither trust nor calculation is possible.

Patriarchal society is fixed on founding fictions from which further falsities were legitimately deduced into the present. Edmund fought pedigreed pretensions with natural truths he will truly or falsely attribute to one who should have spoken them; whether or not the letter was genuine, Edgar *ought to* have offered to share Gloucester's estate with Edmund, Edgar ought to have told his father this, and Gloucester *should* have treated both his sons equally long before Edmund attributed to Edgar words he may have spoken had his right by primogeniture been seriously challenged. Edmund cut himself to make Gloucester recognize his true right by blood. Likewise, it is only after Cain kills Abel that God is moved to place Cain under his protection.

But the chaotic situation in Lear's court not only enlightened Edmund about the truth of sacred power; news of Lear's abrupt departure from Goneril's house and Regan's concomitant visit to Gloucester also involved Edmund's family in a way he could not have foreseen. Now he must go from mischievously bearing false witness against his natural brother, yet a thought experiment that could have led to beneficial results had it made Gloucester treat his two sons equally, to publicly denouncing Edgar as a traitor and parricide. In short, neither Edmund's unfilial thoughts nor his blasphemous words about Nature make him evil. It is by his deeds, first just slanderous words and then truly treacherous acts, that his soul is changed. He could yet have asked pardon from Edgar and Gloucester or fled the scene and still saved his integrity; but the nearing tide of moral chaos makes the chance of windfall profit too alluring. Knowing his father to be the king's man allows him a chance to appear on center stage in the drama with Lear's alluring daughters. Edmund is too proud to seek forgiveness for being envious and then humbly try to crawl back to the moral underground, but he is also too smart not to see evil and too weak to resist its allure. We must not commit the error of viewing Edmund as the master of his dark materials.

But it is first necessary to examine the reason for Lear's departure from Goneril to Regan. We first find Goneril and her steward Oswald discussing her father's bad behavior. She grumbles that while the old king complains incessantly and wrongs her by "flashing into one gross crime or another," his knights "grow riotous." She instructs Oswald to let know that she is unwell and asks that the household "come slack" in the hospitality it used to offer the ex-king and his hundred knights. Goneril claims to have made common cause with her sister over Lear's misbehavior and suggests that she is all but daring him to move to Regan's establishment where he would presumably be treated in the same way. Now describing Lear as an "idle old man" who would claim to govern by the very authority he has given away, she observes that "old men are babes again and must be used with checks as flatteries when they are seen abused." Where she had once used flattery to control Lear, their changed positions now necessitated harsher treatment. Indeed, Goneril even proposes to "breed from" or use these occasions to provoke her father. His two older daughters will be like two furies or rooks on a chessboard as they relentlessly seek to advance the endgame and force checkmate. In this process Edmund, once a mere pawn in the game, will strive with considerable ruthlessness to reach the eighth rank and gain royal status.

Yet Lear is not without pieces on his side. We first see Kent and then the Fool join up with their fallen master and strive to prolong the battle until Cordelia can bring France to save Lear. The question as to whether this will be to England's advantage remains to be pondered over. While some believe Lear to be identical with the very land he has partitioned out, others may feel that England can only be itself after the king is removed. While this issue would be fought out in history over an ugly war some decades later, *King Lear* prophetically explores the main issues at stake.

When exiled Kent disguises himself at mortal risk just to rejoin his ungracious lord, we see some suggestion that King Lear represents more than what he presently is or ever was. Even as Regan says that Lear has ever but slenderly known himself, Kent offers himself as a physician who will come between the self-described dragon and his wrath—though he is first threatened and then severely punished by Lear for this. Should this mad dragon be hailed, healed or hanged? Mad King Charles of France felt that he was made of glass, but even this is more self-reflective. *King Lear* could never have been staged before Elizabeth. Gloriana was more acutely aware than James I that monarchy was essentially a performative role—not held by divine right.

But why then does disguised Kent, offering "service" to his old master, say Lear has "authority" even after he botched his abdication? How does Lear yet have this if he now acts with little reason, no power and opposes authority? Does Kent still serve Lear out of duty or loyalty, or is it that the disgraced noble obeys some intangible charism that cannot be washed off an anointed head? It seems clear that, despite having an uncanny authority which all but silences speech and warps thought about him, Lear is unwilling or unable to control his knights; this harkens to the recent past, when he could not control the jockeying for power between the dukes. In being identical with his presence and actions, Lear is also devoid of interiority; we never hear him in *solus*, see his darker interiority or hear his inner intent. No truly human activity is possible around him. In Edgar's words, "he childed as I fathered"; we only become human in as much as we banish Lear. While not a Falstaff or Caesar, Lear too has the overwhelming presence of a Colossus; when by him we are uncannily aware of his Being in close proximity to our nothingness. Only from here, this abyss, a space of madness and folly, may Lear be safely addressed. This is why his Fool is so vital to Lear's sanity; just as only Yorick could play with Hamlet, so too does Lear need the Fool.

The Fool knows in his heart that Lear is no god; this is why he can talk to him without being silenced or unhinged. When Lear sends for him, shortly after hiring Kent/Caius, the impatient old man is told that the Fool has "much pined away" since Cordelia left for France. While the link between the two is much commented on, and remains both significant and mysterious, it is safe to say that Cordelia's Christ-like love and silence are akin to folly; neither quality can be said to get much ontological support or privation from the old king. Lear's potency is from the Old Testament; he is jealous, given to wrath, and cannot be deterred from passing arbitrary sentences on those he views with ill favor. He often prefers younger children over the older.

Just before the Fool returns, Lear realizes that his commands are being deliberately neglected by Goneril and Albany's household. This "great abatement of kindness" is confirmed when Oswald, asked by Lear who he is, answers "my lady's father." This bitter confirmation that he is now, in substance, *nothing,* moves Lear and Kent to assault the steward even though they must both recognize the futility of their behavior. While Oswald is a rising man, Lear and Kent are on the losing side of history. Kent had earlier called himself, figuratively, Lear's physician, and Caius, his new name, is also that of the short-tempered French doctor in *The Merry Wives of Windsor*. We assume that Kent disguised as Caius will seek to cure or at least care for the diseased Lear.

There are also grounds for assuming that it was Kent who originally persuaded Lear to divide his kingdom. We know from the opening lines of *King Lear* that he was privy to the plan, only surprised by Albany's share not being larger than Cornwall's. Yet he is thunderstruck at Cordelia's abrupt disinheritance by Lear. This would have been the cornerstone of the strategy to prevent war among the dukes and provide for Lear's retirement. It must have been Lear's decision to seek professions of love rather than loyalty, indicative of his sublimated desire for Cordelia and part of his self-stated "darker purpose," that took Kent by surprise. We cannot even deny the possibility that Kent himself would have been a better spouse for Cordelia than either Burgundy or France; such a match between two plain-spoken parties devoted to Lear would have saved the heart of England from foreign rule and assured the old king more security. Indeed, this demi-kingdom then could become the Duchy of Kent. Dover, we note is, also located in the county of Kent.

But jealous Lear cannot give his beloved Cordelia to anyone; this is also the awful key to *Pericles, Prince of Tyre.* This play, attributed to Shakespeare, begins with a sphinxlike riddle that must be solved to win the hand of a princess. Yet the answer points to actual incest between a king and his child. *Pericles* appeared at roughly the same time as *King Lear* and met with great success in Shakespeare's day. We may also note that this reading of *King Lear* makes the strong similarities between Lear and Sophocles' Oedipus even more pronounced. Madness, incestuous desire and self-exile belong together, and the archetypal images of Lear at Dover Beach and Oedipus at Colonus are clearly complementary. Pledging to love Lear only according to her bond, Cordelia withholds Shylock's proverbial pound of flesh. We see why Oswald's calling him "my lady's father" so maddens Lear.

Lear would surely have expected, when he offered Cordelia to Burgundy and France with only a father's curse as dowry, that his daughter would be refused by both her suitors. But the jealous king is confounded when France calls his bluff and takes Cordelia with nothing. Anyone with the remotest knowledge of English history, even if they had not read *King John,* would have known that Cordelia nevertheless possesses a priceless intangible asset: a claim to England's crown. And Cordelia would have surely known this; the fact that she does not refuse to marry France shows that she prefers jeopardizing England's safety to being at her jealous and senile father's mercy. And yet we will see that her heart is yet very deeply divided; Cordelia's unexpected return from France at the head of an army seems to have more to do with Lear than French expansionism.

Upon bidding farewell to her sisters, as France asks her to do, Cordelia assumes that their concern is purely with power and property. This is what she means by saying, "I know what you are." Like many families where a parent has a favorite, the dynamic between the children is defective—especially between the favored child and their siblings. Cordelia must believe what Lear says to her about her sisters; she may never have had a chance to know what they could say of him, or to learn the truth about how they came to be treated unfairly by their sire.

Her sisters hear her request that they love Lear with ill-concealed scorn. She has just insulted them again and persists in acting like their moral superior even after finally losing their father's favor. Goneril replies tartly, urging her to focus on flattering her new husband. They may feel that it was for an unburdened future with her new spouse that Cordelia did not make effusive professions of love similar to theirs, and abandoned Lear. We may possibly suspect that both her suitors had originally told Cordelia they would take her without a dowry before their bluff was called.

In the drama that follows, as we follow Lear's strange journey through mythic space, from the king's near apotheosis on the heath outside Gloucester's castle to a melodramatic conclusion on Dover Beach, this Oedipal thread will serve as a hermeneutic key (or Caius) to interpreting *King Lear.*

But the other dimension to this story, that which is sublime and universal rather than being merely sexual and specific, remains to be fully unpacked. For this to occur we must return to Goneril and see how Lear's demonic rage towards her takes him to the place where God dies. When pious Edgar eventually succeeds Lear, he will always reign in the gigantic shadow cast by his demonic predecessor, and the three distinct aspects of father, king and god will be forever tangled in a toxic trinity of terrifying tension. Only by separating these three persons from each other can human nature be truly redeemed. This sphinx must be faced on Dover Beach.

When his Fool finally appears and offers the king his coxcomb for "banishing" (i.e., freeing) the two daughters who hate him, and only truly banishing she who loves him (yet inadvertently doing her a favor too), Lear threatens to whip him for speaking what they both know to be the truth. The Fool then reminds Lear that he has nothing and can make no use of it. Going on to call Lear a "bitter fool" for ceding his lands, and perhaps chastising Kent as he who advised Lear to do so, the Fool now tells his master that this folly, or the title of fool, is all Lear has left. There is so much folly in the land now that the Fool cannot even describe himself as such anymore.

The Fool makes several references to Lear being caught with his breeches down and his ass exposed. We may suppose these to refer to the illicit sexual passion the old king has revealed by his mad love for Cordelia, but they could also suggest that, since he literally has nothing, he is thus fully present as pure jealous rage. By emptying himself fully, Lear is neither man, king, or even father, but something quite different; he is the powerful living symbol of what never was, or can be, but has haunted the human imagination for a long time. It seemed first that his older daughters were furies who would torture Lear for his sins but we now see that the mad old king reflects the castrated primal father: he embodies the monstrous nightmarish divine fury itself. If Hamlet but blanched before this idea's potential, then Lear will be its fullest actualization. It is as if Cordelia or Christ gelded the old God's destructive power but left his desire unrequited.

For all of his jesting concerning his master's folly in giving everything away and being left with nothing, the Fool did advise Lear to recognize his changed circumstances; now Goneril appears with a sour face to deliver a similar message. Her initial complaint pertains to the disorderly behavior of his knights and she then rather obscurely asks Lear to set them a better example by his own speech and deeds if he does not wish to be held accountable for the same offenses.

This veiled threat is followed by a provocative couplet spoken by the Fool about a foolish sparrow who fed a cuckoo until its head was bitten off. Thus emboldened, Lear asks Goneril if she is his daughter. Upon being told again by her to put away the antics that take him away from his good sense, and being egged on once more by the Fool, he enquires with mock pathos if anyone knows who he is, as he surely is not Lear. When the fool answers that he is now but "Lear's shadow," Lear rhetorically wonders if he has daughters and yet again asks Goneril who she is.

Goneril angrily accuses Lear of allowing his hundred knights to turn her court into a tavern or brothel. She forcefully begs him to reduce his entourage and limit it to men who both know themselves and behave in a fitting manner. Lear responds with fury, calling her a "degenerate bastard." He barks orders to saddle his horses and depart, observing that he still has a daughter. When Albany mildly urges him to be patient, Lear instead hurls a volley of insults at Goneril and claims his train are "men of choice and rarest parts" who both know and fulfill their duty exactly. Lear laments the "small fault" he saw in Cordelia "which ... wrenched his frame of nature from the fixed place, drew from my heart all love and added to the gall." Speaking to himself "O Lear, Lear, Lear" he then beats his head "that led thy folly in and thy dear judgment out." As Albany professes confusion as to what has so moved him, Lear says "it may be so" and curses Goneril.

Emulating Edmund in addressing Nature as his "dear goddess," Lear curses Goneril with sterility, asking she may never have a child who would honor her. If she were to have a child, he wishes it to bring her torment and tears, turning all her pains and benefit to laughter and contempt. He leaves praying she may feel "how much sharper than a serpent's tooth a thankless child is."

Albany, seeing Lear turned from a Sir Toby Belch into an evil raging fury, asks, "Now gods we adore, whereof comes this?" Goneril, surely shaken but knowing Lear better, prudently replies, "Never afflict yourself to know more of it." With Lear having cursed her house and womb, they may be free from all their filial obligations to him, and he can be afforded scope to live out his dotage. We see why few would wish to honor or give sanctuary to a soul, body or spirit of such uncanny spite and horror. But even if this is not who Lear truly is or eventually will be, we should surely join Albany in wishing to know the meaning of the uncanny metamorphosis our souls just beheld.

But to do this, naught but the action of the play can inform our exegesis; in short, good readers will not let actors, characters or ideologies pry their attention from the essence of the drama. While as Lear said, we must shun interpretations "which, like an engine, wrenched my frame of nature from the fixed place, drew from my heart all love, and added to the gall," a critic should also be equally wary of a reading that draws the gall from Lear and leaves him all heart or love.

Lear returns abruptly, complaining that fifty of his followers have already been sent off. Quite ignoring Albany, he tells Goneril her power to make him weep makes him ashamed. Projecting on her the ill-effects of his pride, Lear curses Goneril's every sense, explicitly and roundly, and even threatens his own eyes with plucking out if they betray him again to weep at her causing. Lear tells Goneril that he finds comfort in having another daughter, "kind and comfortable," who will "flay thy wolvish visage" and let him resume the shape she thought he had "cast off forever."

After these terrible maledictions given in the words of the god of generation and genesis, Lear leaves again. Goneril tries to draw Albany's attention to what Lear has just said but he cannot fathom the event. Then after expelling the Fool, addressing him as a knave and not as a fool, she sends Oswald to Regan with news of what has taken place and her own "particular fear." We may see that the Fool has indeed been as much as a provocateur as jester and has told Lear of Oswald's mission. This justifies Goneril in her suspicion of Lear as well. Giving a hundred knights to a man in his dotage merely provides a hundred reasons for offended pride to threaten them. While Albany still prefers to trust, Lear's speech towards her shows Goneril to be in the right.

Lear meanwhile dispatches Kent/Caius to Gloucestershire, presumably to Cornwall and Regan's residence, giving news of his fight with Goneril to Regan and short notice of his new plans to stay with her. He would do this only if he feared that Goneril would get her version of events to Regan before he gets to her. He goes to Regan, although the Fool, who left Goneril just after she called Oswald, mocks him for thinking Regan will treat him any better. The Fool hints that he has a nose for what Lear cannot or will not see. Lear can neither see himself nor see how his older daughters see him. If we hear Lear mutter "I did her wrong" while the Fool mocks him for not seeing that his older daughters think alike, we must wonder if he means Goneril or Cordelia. His later musings, "so kind a father" and "monstrous ingratitude," suggest that it is Cordelia. And while Lear is both too proud and has no way of reaching her, his courier Kent/Caius has a signed letter explaining his plight. It is possible that as Kent makes the long ride from Albany to Gloucester, a copy of this letter could be sent to France. The link between Caius and Cordelia is now Lear's only hope.

While we already anticipated some of it in discussing Edmund's framing of Edgar, the pivotal theme of *King Lear*'s Act II is the quarrel between the two messengers from Goneril's castle. Which messenger is trustworthy and who bears perfidy from Albion? In short, what is the truth about Lear? Is Goneril but another version of Lady Macbeth or does she know her own father for what he is? While we know that Goneril's account was accepted by the other half of Lear's divided land, perhaps the true recipient of his appeal was not Regan but Cordelia, despite this not being Lear's explicit intention. The message preached to the outcasts or Gentiles was heard, while his own knew him not. But is this echo of the gospel's fate a perverse parody? Is the truth owned by the law and the legitimate or by the lettered but illegitimate? Did God stand up for bastards?

Act II begins, as earlier noted, with Edmund finding out that Cornwall and Regan are visiting the Earl of Gloucester. But he also hears of "likely wars" between the two dukes. Although Curran, his source, may have thought that Regan would take arms against Goneril for Lear's sake, and this would not have been consistent with what Edmund saw of the amity between the sisters, the news still pointed towards a situation where his connections, intelligence and unscrupulous ways would be of value to one side or another in this conflict; nature has heard his prayers and now he must act swiftly and ruthlessly. Despite a certain queasiness about doing something he had only contemplated but never done before, he now takes steps to convince his credulous old father that Edgar is a treacherous patricide. After trying to see if Edgar had said anything at all against either of the dukes, for Edmund like almost everybody in *King Lear* is not an omniscient observer, Edmund proceeds to set up a situation where Edgar would seem to be fleeing after unsuccessfully trying to force Edmund to join him in killing their father; wounding himself adds a touch of realism to the bastard's treachery against his own blood. Gloucester is easily duped.

Edmund skillfully puts the best arguments against the implausibility of the scenario he has just set up in his own brother's mouth; why would anyone believe a bastard who would profit so much by displacing the legitimate heir? Here Gloucester falls into the trap by bringing up the earlier evidence of the forged letter; it never occurs to him that Edmund forged it himself. It is essential that the earl and his heir never meet to discuss this letter or who it was that pitted each against the other. Edmund has created a situation where father and heir both fear each other too much to ever meet. Indeed, Gloucester now seeks Cornwall's permission to place a price on Edgar's head. Once a state of war is established, and vile deeds of fear or hostility have been performed by both parties, it is much harder for either to question their conflict's origins. All this is natural to Edmund the Bastard, who has lived his whole life in a state of undeclared war of all against all. At the very least, he has exposed these two entitled nobles to his outlaw reality.

Cornwall and Regan now appear and Gloucester introduces them to Edmund his loyal younger son. While Edgar, as Lear's godson, was seen with prejudice by the power couple, and craftily associated with Lear's hundred knights, Edmund, his accuser, is identified as the kind of man who will be of use in the fight against Lear; his loyalty is swiftly sought by and pledged to them.

We next meet Kent and Oswald. After their messages were delivered to Regan they followed her separately to Gloucester's house. It is here that Kent/Caius resumes hostilities with the bewildered steward. His behavior is odd unless he is deliberately trying to make Regan and Cornwall declare themselves for one side or the other; this strategy would also match our suspicion that he has already been in touch with Cordelia about Lear's altered circumstances.

Kent's truly unpleasant behavior towards Oswald, a man who has done him no harm, reflects quite unpleasantly on the way unconditional loyalty can affect behavior; it stands in striking contrast to the calculating conduct of Edmund. Each man is equally unnatural in his actions, but Kent clearly goes out of his way to give offense. Like abdicated Lear, he seems to want

to have it both ways, giving up his title but yet behaving towards commoners as if he were still an earl. Even in claiming privilege as Lear's man, he
forgets or ignores that the ex-king is now Goneril's inferior. And disguised
Caius has no status at all; he is but a nobody who behaves like a ruffian.

After next insulting Cornwall, Kent is finally placed in the stocks. He
has deserved this penalty by demonstrating that his poor manners and ugly
speech are not natural but exaggerated and contrived. Even if Gloucester
huffs a bit and expresses his disapproval of the duke's action, the fact remains that Cornwall and Regan are the absolute rulers of their half of England, regardless of whether Kent (or Caius) likes it or not. Kent's exposure
to the elements is a preview of what lies in store for Lear; neither of them
seems to have any idea of what it means to be a nobody.

But Kent has a surprise up his sleeve that may explain his hubristic behavior. He has a letter from Cordelia; his claim that she has been told of
his "obscured course" suggests it was Kent himself who sent her Lear's epis-
tle and named his next stop. But he will do more than bring it all to a head
so Lear's enemies could be foiled. In his eyes, this short spell in the stocks
is like a vicarious martyrdom with Kent, the lesser of the king's two bodies,
sure in the hope of freeing resurrection and a reward/martyr's crown/ducal
coronet after a few hours of suffering. Just as Paul claimed that Christ spoke
through him, it is Lear's sacred body suffering in the stocks in Kent. Like
James I, moreover, Lear is the physical form of the Old Testament God-
King's two natures.

If Lear symbolizes the God of the Old Testament then, most surely,
He is One. This is consistent with Lear being the monarch of a realm united
under him by war. As we noted, the rulers under him, Albany and Cornwall, who represent the geographical extremities of the land, are dukes, literally warlords; there were no dukes left when Elizabeth died. The last, the
Duke of Norfolk, was executed in 1571. It was with James' accession that
his sons became the Dukes of Cornwall and Albany respectively.

This shows how Lear, having unified England, is a warlord, or even a
Messiah like David, in the eyes of someone like Kent. The king's hundred
knights would have been like the young men who fought alongside David.
Kent by this analogy is like Joab, King David's *consigliere*. This military
background explains why Kent was so offended that Oswald, a civilian,
wore a sword. We can also now see clearly why the presence of a hundred

killers in her own house would not please Goneril; in her words: "a hundred knights: yes, that on any dream, each buzz, each fancy, each complaint, dislike, he may enguard his dotage with their powers and hold our lives at mercy." But if Kent, both Joab and Jeremiah in his own heated imagination, expects Lear to arrive at the head of an army to deliver his suffering servant and vanquish his enemies, he is badly mistaken.

Meanwhile, in striking contrast to the grandiose scenario imagined by Kent's angry imagination, Edgar, the next king of England, is anointing himself in mud and dirt. This proclaimed outlaw is thus forced to "take the basest and most poorest shape that ever penury, in contempt of man, brought near to beast," and claim to be from Bedlam. As Bedlam is a contraction of Christ's birthplace, England's anointed Messiah will be this strange beast shambling from Bethlehem.

But all this is unknown to Lear and Kent, king and messenger or god and prophet, when they are reunited at the stocks before Gloucester's residence. Lear, first bewildered at not meeting Kent with a response to his message to Regan, is infuriated by Kent's punishment: "Tis worse than murder to do upon respect such violent outrage." But when prudently asked if he did anything to deserve this, Kent says that as his letters were ignored in favor of those Oswald brought, he "drew, having more man than wit about me." Kent's response totally neglects to mention the rude and disorderly lengths to which he went to insult both Oswald and Cornwall; yet again, it seems as if he wants to provoke his choleric and jealous king to quarrel with Regan.

Then, as his Fool continues mocking his folly in giving all to his two daughters, Lear complains of a hysterical passion climbing up his insides and then goes alone to the house. He leaves behind a gentleman who asks Caius if he gave any more offense than that he spoke of. Kent says "none" and asks in turn, "How chance the king comes with so small a number?" The Fool tells him he deserves the stocks for so foolish a query:

That sir which serves and seeks for gain
  And follows but for form,
Will pack when it begins to rain
  And leave thee in the storm.
But I will tarry; the fool will stay,

And let the wise man fly.
The knave turns fool that runs away;
The fool no knave, pardie.

The Fool is loyal to Lear from folly. But as his job is to restore Lear's humanity, and since his loyalty makes him continually rekindle Lear's choleric identity, we may ask: is humanity Lear's essence? Does the Fool recognize this abiding anger issue? Is he but one who says in his heart there is no God, a man who dispenses cynical wisdom for a godless world?

Lear now returns with Gloucester; despite raging at Cornwall's feigned excuses for being unable to meet him, he still cannot admit to himself that Regan and Cornwall are aligned with hated Goneril. But even though he threatens to beat their chamber door down until they have speech with him, the duke and Regan finally appear only when Goneril herself is conveniently nearby.

After Kent is silently released, and a few pleasantries are exchanged, Lear swiftly tells Regan how evil Goneril is: "sharp-toothed unkindness like a vulture...." She responds urging patience and suggesting that Goneril knows her duty better than Lear knows. Going on to claim that if Goneril restrained his riotous followers, she was blameless for this, Regan tells Lear that he is very old and must be ruled by those who know him better than he knows himself. But if, as she said earlier, he "ever but slenderly knew himself," it follows that Lear has ever been, at least in her view, a natural slave. This is why she urges him to return to Goneril and admit he wronged her. When Lear then admits to being old and begs on his knees that she promise him "raiment, bed and food," Regan asks him again to cease these "unsightly tricks" and return to her sister.

Rising up Lear refuses, repeating his complaint that Goneril halved his train. He then proceeds to curse his oldest daughter again with the very poisonous serpent tongue he had accused her of wounding him with. Invoking the heavens, he curses her bones with lameness, wishes her eyes be struck with lightning, and then asks the fens to infect her beauty so it may fall and blister.

When Regan swears that he would wish her evils in the same way when the mood struck him, Lear says that she will never earn his curse. He tries to contrast the sisters and insists she would not grudge his pleasures, halve his train or "oppose the bolt" to his coming in. Lear claims she better knows "offices of nature, bond of childhood, effects of courtesy, dues of gratitude," and pointedly reminds Regan of the half of the kingdom he gave her. When she tersely asks him to get to the point, perhaps having a quite different memory of the happy childhood memories he has created for her, Lear changes the subject and asks instead, "who put my man in the stocks?"

We must note that Regan herself has also dodged facing Lear's main point that she owes him a place for his entire entourage since he gave her half his realm. But yet Lear's plaint has been that he and his train must be indulged, bad behavior and all, because of his gift. Both prefer to avoid discussion of the semi-coerced context in which this gift was offered, solicited, and made. The real issue seems to be the size of his entourage. But while Lear approaches this indirectly by asking about Kent's treatment, Regan prefers to wait until Goneril arrives. This must have been her choice all along, but it would have been even harder to sustain when Lear brought the past up.

But now, just as the trumpet blast announces Goneril's arrival, Lear's wrath turns to Oswald. Associating him with Goneril and his humiliations at her house, the old man dismisses the steward as an upstart slave. Asked to explain this seemingly random blast of rage, he then returns to the stocks, demanding Regan admit that Caius was not punished at her behest. While his angry meanderings are connected, his audience cannot see how they make sense.

However, the actual presence of Goneril, his *bete noire*, focuses Lear's mad wrath on her. He is horrified to see Regan take her sister's hand, seeing it rightly as an explicit sign that they are not afraid to let Lear see their alliance against him. Is Goneril not ashamed to see his beard? At her cold reply that his indiscreet dotage takes offense needlessly, he turns again to the stocks. When Cornwall takes responsibility for this and adds that Caius deserved much worse, Lear is inclined to pursue the matter further, but he is checked when Regan, perhaps emboldened by Goneril's presence, says more forcefully that "being weak, he should be so." She offers to accept him if he returns to Goneril for the month and then comes to her after dismissing half his train. She yet mouths the flimsy pretext of not being prepared to entertain him but sticks to her guns.

Lear recoils in horror at this, listing three things he would prefer over going back to Goneril: living in the open with the wolf and owl, begging for shelter from "hot-blooded France" who took his other yet unnamed daughter without dower, or even being slave to detested Oswald. When Goneril notes that this is his choice, Lear, struggling to keep his equanimity, asks her not to "make him mad." What he earlier called hysteria is now named correctly: madness. This is the violent arbitrary power Lear had once ruled all England by, since all men had feared it; but with approaching senility it now threatens to escape the limits of his ego and destroy him.

Still struggling for continence Lear bids farewell to Goneril, saying he will never see her again. His parting words call her a disease in his flesh or sin in his blood he must admit to. Lear will not judge her; he leaves this to heaven and will not even warn against its judgment though he urges her to mend what she can and be better. He and his hundred knights will stay with Regan. But his hope to escape madness by living with Regan are dashed when she pleads unreadiness. He must go to Goneril; while his hysterical reason is mixed with passion, she knows what she does.

Now the two daughters unite against Lear; in ironic imitation of his coercive love auction, they keep reducing the number of knights he needs, as each bids lower than the other. Indeed, the more they love him the less help they will accept from others; this as we suspected was what Lear would have expected had his nursery been with Cordelia, as originally planned. What was a hundred and is now fifty soon becomes twenty-five, before dropping to ten, five, one and finally stopping at the dreaded nothing. His daughters argue most logically that a house divided against itself cannot stand; a smaller number is easier to control in case of disobedience.

Lear self-pityingly cries, "I gave you all," only for Regan to reply, "and in good time you gave it." Then, despairing at Regan's limit of twenty-five, and observing "those wicked creatures yet do look favored when others are more wicked," he says to cursed Goneril, "I'll go with thee, thy fifty yet doth double five and twenty and thou art twice her love," only to hear, "what need you five and twenty? ten? or five … in a house where twice so many have a command to tend you?"

Lear's words, "O reason not the need! Our basest beggars are in the poorest thing superfluous" are soon refuted by his weakness before the storm. Far from being the result of tragic pathos, they rather show an ignorance of common life only matched by lack of self-knowledge. Unable,

due to the mad energy by which he accumulated it, to turn his massive accumulation of power into love, Lear turns bad theologian when he says that
true need is not material but measured by patience. While showing a
hubristic lack of humility in likening himself to a poor old man, stricken
by both grief and age, he cries out to the gods who may have given his
daughters the power to treat him so unnaturally; no longer seeking patience,
he seeks vengeful anger; rather than let tears stain his cheeks, Lear's revenges
must be the terror of the earth. His mad choice of toxic maddening rage
over tearful humility must not be admired, emulated or found sublime.

Even if they seem callous, and their later behavior shows them to be in
many respects Lear's daughters, Goneril and Regan do not act imprudently
when their maddened father storms out into the terrible thunder and rain.
They feel that he, for once, should taste the consequences of his mad raging
folly; furthermore, there is no space to house Lear's troublesome followers:
"He is attended with a desperate train, and what they may incense him to,
being apt to have his ear abused, wisdom bids fear." Kent and the Fool are
both effective instigators of strife even before loyally joining their powers
with Lear, who still has a warlord's charisma and for whom they have near
religious devotion. The pair are also deeply devoted to Cordelia and it is
arguable that it is for the sake of restoring her to power that they abuse
Lear's ear. But that would lead to the deposition of Goneril and Regan and
brew a truly dangerous political storm for all England.

Act III begins with a reminder that Lear is minded as "unquietly" as
the "foul weather." Having stormed out of Gloucester's house, into the
thunder and rain outside, he seems to have made common cause with the
turbulent elements and mentally metamorphosed into the storm god of
Genesis and the Flood. While this anticipates the character of Prospero in
significant ways, the eponymous character in *King Lear* is not even remotely
in control of either himself or the awful weather that surrounds him. Yet
we do see how identifying with the storm helps the deranged man to pre-
tend to himself, and those who believe in him, that an anointed king is a
sublime force, quite distinct from both the shivering physical body being
soaked by the storm and the demented brain now in danger of being permanently unhinged by its lack of self-knowledge.

But even as Lear and the Fool strut and fret madly across the soaking
sheets of sleet as they impersonate El Shaddai and Ecclesiastes, Kent/Caius

is hard at work. He is both spreading wild rumors of dissent between the Dukes of Albany and Cornwall, as well as preparing the way for the invasion force from France he has requested from Cordelia. Calling his old king "kind" is part of arguing that his violent grace is not bound by ethics or morality. It is beyond doubt that such a restoration would constitute a treasonous undertaking. We should always remember that any depiction of an invasion of England, especially from the old enemy France, would have been guaranteed to meet a hostile response from a justifiably paranoid English audience. The fact of Lear's delusional dementia is also relevant. English kings could not be seen as figureheads; this was just why Lear first decided to abdicate. But he could not be replaced by a French queen.

Yet Lear in his senility strikingly signifies the worst qualities of the Old Testament god. He is self-righteous, genocidal, and jealously obsessed with sex, infidelity and fertility. Detaching his own aged suffering human aspect from this hubristic hyper-Uranian vantage point permits the most awful judgment to be passed on humanity; all will follow him into the abyss once the rainbow dividing the waters above from those below is removed. The promise made to Noah is broken; he had no daughters to betray him— where were they when he was naked and asked for shelter? Nature's molds must crack and thunder should strike flat the great globe itself before his wrath.

As with *King John,* a king goes into exile, travelling hopelessly across his flooded lands while a French invasion, invited by his own lords, lands welcomed and unopposed at Dover. But there are also striking differences between the two scenarios that shed further light on the meaning of *King Lear.* Just as the political issues between John and the barons, even though the Magna Carta was not as significant then as it is now, were pointedly ignored in *King John,* the theological overtones of *King Lear,* too dangerous to be even spoken of before delusional James I, are on overt literally naked display.

What looked so sublime and beautiful from the lofty perch of the all highest, all-maker and all-destroyer becomes cruel and evil if Edmund's is a legitimate viewpoint, i.e., if the proper point of perspective is the hovel and not the heavens. In short, if the ultimate unit by which benefit is accounted is an individual conscious soul, and not the creator and or destroyer, these multiple realities occasion a Copernican shift in reality; Lear's world becomes the Real World.

In his madness, Lear does not curse the fierce elements; they were merely harnessed by him when he, like Job's God, created the land. The wickedness and ingratitude of his children is the cause of the masterwork wrought by his fiery will disintegrating; as they have marred it, putting the parts back to their primal place of origin is a producer's final prerogative and pleasure. But yet he must mildly chastise the heavens for taking his daughter's side when they include his old body in their universal judgment upon the earth. Lear brazenly calls himself "a man more sinned against than sinning." This is like a cynical statesman calling his evils "acts of state" and not sins.

The shift in emphasis from God's greatness to human goodness is at the heart of Shakespeare's project; this change is reflected in *King Lear* when the mad king notes that his "wits begin to turn" and actually finds "one place in my heart that's sorry yet" for his faithful fool. Yet this "turn" back to the cave or hovel by Lear cannot be taken to imply resurrection or restoration; *King Lear* must not be read by monarchists or virtuoso actors in a way that denies its deep humanism—this would deny its truth and profundity. The turn is ontological, not comic in a way requiring a happy ending where Lear presides like Prospero over the wedding of Cordelia to Edgar; his landing is hard. An occasional moment of love or lucidity cannot break the downward path of senility. A possibly nihilistic shift from a world with an omnipotent god, however willful, in his heaven, to a new place where we must seek thunder's cause ourselves, and own that too much in life is invisibly made or random, will cause new kinds of madness and moral blindness. But it must be made.

A chief risk or madness illustrated in *King Lear* and very much present in our time has to do with family values, sentimentality or crass selfishness replacing religion, reason and patriotism. As we now see, Gloucester decides to choose loyalty to Lear, partially supported by compassion, above his responsibility to protect England from France. The very fact that he cannot even speak of this seditious matter to Edmund, but instead merely alludes to the dangerous content of the letter locked in his closet, is suggestive. We can also see that he has involved Edmund in this risky matter, presuming on his loyalty, without asking his consent. The fact that Edmund has already decided to betray Gloucester, even before reading the letter which would give him good cause to prefer nation over family, merely shows that his own priorities are opportunistic. Having chosen nature as his goddess, it is natural that "the younger rises when the old doth fall." There is no more necessity in moral deduction; choices are inductively made by rootless individuals. In short, what could be vertiginous is the fact that ethical criteria or procedures no longer exist; this, in a sense, prefigures what Gloucester will learn when he faces the moral abyss at Dover.

Meanwhile Lear, Kent and the Fool have found a hovel where they can take shelter from the tyranny of nature. That this position is also a moral hovel, low but sturdy, where they must finally reason by need rather than vanity, is suggested by Lear's first refusal to stoop to enter it. He claims that this will break his heart. He goes on to explain that the storm's merely physical discomfort will distract him from the tempest in his mind when it turns towards the treatment he suffered from his daughters. Far worse than the storm is knowing that Regan and Goneril would allow their "old kind father, whose frank heart gave all," to go out on such a night. This is the stated reason why he urges the "boys" to go in, adding for himself, "I'll pray, and then I'll sleep."

But this concern for his boys, under the rough tutelage of the natural elements, now suddenly extends to cover all without shelter: "Poor naked wretches, wheresoe'er you are that bide the pelting of this pitiless storm, how shall your houseless heads and unfed sides, your looped and windowless raggedness, defend you from seasons such as these? O, I have taken too little care of this." This kinder Lear will not refuse to "reason by need" or priggishly see man as not living "by bread alone but by the word of God." Lear declares that "pomp," the wealthy and privileged, must "take physic" and "expose" itself "to feel what wretches feel." The wealthy are then obliged to "shake the superflux," and share their riches so that they may "show the heavens more just." But this radical moment of revelation, which amounts to nothing less than a call for the redistribution of power and riches, is halted by the Fool. He has just met disguised Edgar in the hovel, and the strange appearance of the very subject of Lear's speech now demands his godfather's avid attention.

In a strange parody of a Platonic dialogue between a king and a philosopher, the very two who must plan how to create a perfect state where wealth is fairly divided and the gods are shown to be just, a mad ex-king and a disguised, outlawed, ex-courtier strip naked and talk nonsense. Tom is both the thing itself, a "poor, bare, forked animal," and the wisdom that comes from an ex-courtier stripping all false appearances from his soul so that justice is its own reward. And while much of the dialogue justly passes as nonsense, seeing a once great king mad, naked, and longing for love like anyone else is surely a vivid lesson for England's next ruler. We also see that the ideal community is one where power is not had by hereditary right, and parents cannot recognize their progeny. The families of Lear and Gloucester give fine negative examples why. It is also striking how the dialogue's end is hidden; after calling him "philosopher," "Athenian" and "Theban," Lear takes Edgar to the cave to keep talking. Lear's own senile mind may not hold the insight it just gained but he somehow saw his heir and godson and may have given it to him.

But back in the real world of power and profit, Cornwall is reassuring a disingenuous Edmund that his preference of loyalty (to him) over blood is ultimately justified by the badness of both Gloucester and Edgar. This being the case, it is merit for Edmund to be provoked by what is bad. As Edmund goes on to bewail the malicious fortune that led him to find Gloucester's complicity with French interests, Cornwall says that this very intelligence, whether true or false, has made Edmund the new Earl of Gloucester; it has given the duke a pretext to move against Lear's man Gloucester and replace him with someone ruthless and loyal to his side in the power struggle.

By betraying his father, Edmund has given Cornwall indubitable proof of his loyalty; for this the duke promises the Bastard that he shall "find a dearer father" in his love. Even if Edmund privately admits to feeling the conflict in his blood, he hopes to find his father "comforting the king." That would "stuff his suspicion more fully," refuting the suspicion Edmund had forged the incriminating letters, and surely hasten his untainted elevation to the earldom of Gloucester.

The scene shifts to an unspecified locale on Gloucester's estate as Gloucester is just leaving. He promises to make Lear more comfortable on his return, even as Kent reports, "all the power of his wits have given way to his impatience." As Lear, Edgar/Tom and the Fool enter talking more nonsense it is clear that the king's raging dementia has worsened, perhaps under the Fool's influence; Lear now seeks to conduct a trial of his two daughters. Even as Edgar warns Lear against being "an angler in a sea of darkness" like Nero, of hunting for impurity when not free of sin himself, the king sets up a mad tribunal, with Tom and the Fool as co-judges beside Caius, to try his two cruel daughters. While we do not know if objects or beasts stood in place of Goneril and Regan, the ensuing masque or spectacle is grotesque enough for Edgar to weep beneath his madman's disguise.

While the king now mercifully goes to sleep, Gloucester returns to tell that he has overheard news of a plot of death against Lear. Because of this, he has prepared a litter to take him to Dover where there will be welcome and protection. He warns that there is no time to lose; a half hour's delay could result in Lear's capture and death, along with that of all of his party.

As the Fool, Kent and Gloucester hurry Lear away, Tom/Edgar is deemed supernumerary and left behind to muse on what he has just seen. As befits the king's philosopher, Edgar realizes now that all private griefs somehow dwindle at the recognition that one is not alone in misery. The infinite sorrows of the literal idiot or isolated man diminish when we see they are held in common with suffering humanity; this broader perspective somehow frees the soul from the crushing weight of isolated loneliness, an absurd burden that nobody can, should or ought to bear: "the mind much sufferance doth o'erskip, when grief has mates and bearing fellowship."

Thinking only now of imperiled and divided England, rather than lamenting his own diminished prospects, its next king thus shows impersonal concern for the common good and "showing the heavens more just." In setting aside his personal pride, as Lear or the Old Testament God could not, "how light and portable my grief seems now, when that which makes me bend, makes the king bow," exiled Edgar somehow finds in himself unexpected strength and greatness of soul. His unaccommodated state has preserved him from the commodious evils of Hobbesian ethics.

And even more mysteriously this power has come from Lear: "he childed as I fathered." In short, the old king and his successor and godson somehow, by the magic of mantic madness, mutually grant and receive a mandate to rule England. Even as Lear entered senile second childhood, he still hailed Edgar as a philosopher, not the wretch others thought he was, and thus helped his godson become a man. Even literally, Lear's being reduced to senility by his own daughters, and thus "childed," matches the way Edgar ends in disinheritance, having been "fathered" by Gloucester. All this being so, Edgar sees he must ignore false appearances and act so that innocent valor will vindicate his tarnished name. For now, he'll hide or "lurk" and pray for the safety of "the king." First, the evil afflicting the land, for which King Lear is scarcely innocent, must burn itself out.

This terrifying process really swings into motion when old Gloucester, after having successfully managed the removal of Lear to Dover, is designated for punishment by Cornwall and Regan. When Edmund is detached from him, and sent off with Goneril by Cornwall, he knows full well that they intend to take revenge on his father not fit for his beholding and does nothing to stop it. The immediate cause of this violence is news of the landing of a French army on English soil; it is easy to see that an English audience, especially in Shakespeare's justifiably paranoid time, would not be well disposed to those on the side of any such incursion. The tension between this and sympathy for the sacred person of a king pervades *King Lear*. And yet, the overt use of torture to preserve public safety or to punish a party suspected with good reason of instigating or working with these invaders, will not be *looked* well upon. But are there some necessary but violent acts for our own good that we would rather not see, or are they evil and thus *verboten*?

If we are to draw inferences about his nature by his illegitimate fathering and later neglect of Edmund, superstitious old Gloucester seems to be the kind of person who is ruled by his senses rather than his conscience. The safety of a senile king matters more to him than the danger to England from invasion. Too easily led and deceived by visual evidence, physical pleasures, and feelings, the earl does not seem to have much moral interiority; "out of sight is out of mind" sums up the kind of outlook that led to his leaving dangerously incriminating evidence around, or within the grasp of a love-child he had earlier treated in just such a way. Abstract ideas like patriotism or loyalty do not move him very much but the overt violation of his hospitality by Cornwall and Regan, his feudal superiors since they have inherited Wales and the West while Goneril and Albany have Scotland and the North, surely does, as does Edmund/Edgar's claim that aged fathers should share lands equally with their children, after the king's own example.

For all these reasons, it could be said that Gloucester did meet some form of rough justice at Cornwall's hands. But the terrifying literary symmetry between punishment and crime in *King Lear*, which Edgar later comments on, must mean that this is not the duke's work but the Bard's. In other words, we are meant to see in Gloucester's brutal blinding the justice of the heavens. But how far does the range of this sublime justice extend? To Goneril and Regan and Edmund, to be sure, but does it include their father, the king himself? And what of the old god who looks like him?

Yet these issues must be tabled for a while as we return to the grotesque event of Gloucester's blinding. Even if he like Oedipus had symbolically been blind, and his physical penalty enacts a psychic truth for all to see, its agent acted from spite though he likely saw the moral symmetry of his deed. If Gloucester's evil was banal, and not undeserved, Cornwall's malice is deliberate. For this reason, his killing by one of his own men is also just; even if, like Gloucester, the servant acted in ignorance of the full context, he responded rightly to his master's overt malice. Justice must not only be done, it also should be seen to be done. Torturing the earl was rough justice but it was unnecessary to blind him; imprisonment would have been well sufficient to the case.

This action also displays evil's contagious nature; that is why some say that ugly but necessary acts of justice must not be seen. Overt violence attracts some and repels others in a way that only reveals if their moral disposition is passive or active, not good or evil. Gloucester's passive-aggressive attitude when apprehended by Cornwall and Regan may have to do with stalling for more time for Lear to escape, while he is likely being tortured, but it also inflames their anger. He protests the letters were not from a foe but a "neutral heart" and does not mention Cordelia.

When Gloucester finally blurts out that he let Lear escape because he would not see Regan pluck out Lear's eyes or watch Goneril tear him apart, he is still temporizing. He will focus their rage on him while not answering the repeated query why Lear was sent to Dover. He goes on to blame them for not opening their gates to Lear, while not mentioning that the king never asked to be admitted; Gloucester ends promising to see "winged vengeance overtake such children."

These words lead Cornwall to blind him in one eye. The duke asks the earl if he now sees "Vengeance" and, as we touched on earlier, one of Cornwall's lifelong servants is moved to bid him stop. When, calling the servant "dog," Regan asks his intent, he threatens to pluck her beard, "if she had one," as she treated Gloucester. As servant and master draw their swords and fight, taking "the chance of anger," Regan now treacherously intervenes by stabbing the servant in the back and killing him. As the servant falls, he cries out that Gloucester still has an eye to see mischief overtake the wicked, but the mortally wounded Cornwall plucks out his other eye so the earl may not see this just outcome.

As Gloucester now despairing in blindness cries out for Edmund to avenge him, Cornwall, with almost his last dying breath, taunts him with the vile revelation that Edmund, "who is too good to pity thee," had betrayed him. Now seeing in his blindness that "Edgar was abused," Gloucester is put out to the gates, but not before asking pardon from Edgar and blessing him. Cornwall, having denied Gloucester sight of justice, now succumbs to his wound as his other servants ponder this event. Convinced Regan will not live long either if there is any justice, they leave to go after Gloucester and have "the Bedlam" guide him. They do not know he is Edgar.

Edgar himself, oblivious to the events going on in his father's house, is pondering fate. Things seem to have passed him by. A cautious philosopher, he chose not to make himself known to the king's men before his father and is Poor Tom again. Valuing safety over truth or virtue, he consoles himself with the conceit that it may be best to be at the bottom of Fortune's wheel, without even the flattery of a mad king; without hope there is no fear of falling lower. But then he sees the earl, looking much the worse for wear, guided towards him by an even older man.

Edgar hears Gloucester send the old man away, saying that even though he cannot see his way, he has no way and thus does not need eyes; further, since he stumbled when he saw, he was even blinder then. Gloucester now sees that while prosperity filled him with false knowledge of things, he was blind to what was more important; misery has taught him far better. He now laments that if he could touch his dear son Edgar, it would be as good as having eyes again.

At this, Edgar says to himself that no one can say "I am at the worst," since he feels even worse now. We note that he feels no joy either at Gloucester's punishment or even at his vindication in his father's heart. He merely observes that as long as we can say "this is the worst," the worst has not yet befallen us. This must mean that even the worst personal state can be made worse by terrible things befalling those we love. These words surely reveal Edgar's generous spirit.

We find that Gloucester, made aware of Tom's presence, wants to be guided by him. Since he sees better, hearing the intuitions of his soul better than egotistic instincts or sensual impulses, the deposed earl rejects the objection that Tom is a beggar and madman, pointing out that he must have "reason" to have survived last night's storm when Gloucester saw one like him who made him "think a man a worm," yet also brought his son to mind. His mind then was "scarce friends with him" but he admits now to have "heard more." Yet now follow his oft-quoted words: "As flies to wanton boys are we to th' gods; / They kill us for their sport." Their context is rarely recalled. But even if these words do not express Shakespeare's feelings, they show Gloucester, their speaker, to be in a religious despair. But yet, this does not cause him to become selfish towards others; as we will see, he does not feel that nothing is forbidden after faith or trust in a good God dies.

Edgar is now deeply conflicted about how to interact with his father. While part of him craves to find more about what has happened to Gloucester, he yet feels constrained to stay within the identity of Mad Tom, particularly while the old man is still there. Saying to himself, "bad is the trade that must play fool to sorrow, angering self and others," Edgar yet blesses Gloucester. The earl now brushes aside the old man's misgivings about leaving him with a naked madman; his concern, most Christian, is with clothing Tom's naked body; while not saying so, it is as if he were providing for his Edgar. It is also fitting, "the time's plague, when madmen lead the blind." Gloucester dismisses the old man, first saying "Do as I bid thee." He then amends this: "or rather, do thy pleasure." He will no longer speak as the older man's feudal lord and order him around.

Left alone with his father, Edgar still struggles with the question of how best to dress his naked identity. Finally remaining by default as Poor Tom, he admits to knowing the way to Dover. His father now hands him his purse; this is also a symbolic act since he believes the naked madman to be one whom "the heavens' plagues / Have humbled to all strokes." In other words, his deed says "blessed are the meek." This pagan enactment of the values of the beatitudes suggests that they are natural, and erotic, not commanded by god; Gloucester's acts are no longer ruled by divine commerce or human commodity. Even if "the heavens deal so still" that the poor man finds happiness out of the wretchedness of the rich when they fall, it is just. Once more echoing Lear's insight, he wishes that "the superfluous and lust-dieted man who slaves your ordinance, that will not see because he does not feel" meaning the spoiled and wealthy who contort the law to their own benefit, "feel your power quickly." He clearly means that this great social revolution must come soon: "so distribution should undo excess and each man have enough." Gloucester ends again asking the way towards Dover and a high cliff that seems to mirror the contiguous and dizzying inequalities between high and low. He wishes to be led to its very brim where he "will repair all the misery thou dost bear." The earl is blind to what he says but his son yet gives him his arm. While his intention is clear, it is not certain how Edgar will react to his sire's suicidal strategy.

Meanwhile even as Lear and Gloucester, the one mystically and the other mindfully, see the error of their past ways and seek refuge in senility and self-destruction, respectively, the next generation of rulers pursue their own extreme reactions to these events. When Goneril and Edmund return North, so as to unify their forces to meet the French invasion, they are met by Oswald who tells them that the Duke of Albany has "changed" remarkably. Goneril's husband is all smiles to hear of the French army's arrival and is not pleased to have news of her return. When told by Oswald of Gloucester's "treachery" to their cause and of Edmund's "loyalty," he chastised the steward "for turning the wrong side out"; Albany finds pleasant what he ought to dislike most and deems offensive what he should like. This distaste surely extends to Goneril herself.

His wife's reaction is one of disgust more than surprise. Goneril calls Albany "cowish," despising him for the meek deference he shows towards her senile father. Here the issue has to do with whether Lear's authority is timeless and divine or ultimately timebound and now demented; we recall that we are in Reformation England; any move by a king to claim divine right smacked too much of the corruptly idolatrous papacy to those who had a congregational or republican view of religion. And since the parties of religious reform and changeless divine right, low and high church, had been at odds since the days of Henry VIII, we cannot take it for granted that Lear's person would be held sacred by *King Lear*'s audience or readers, though this is surely Albany's view. Yet even the low church puritans, while angrily denying any identification of an infallible pope or sacred king with God himself, very much believed in the angry and almighty deity of the Old Testament. Only mad Lear, blind Gloucester, and, we must imagine,

Shakespeare, seem to have reached a very different view of God. This outlook, stressing love and charity, harkens to the egalitarian views of Jesus and the New Testament as translated and interpreted by Erasmus.

But this Renaissance Christian humanism, perhaps still conceivable in *via media* Elizabethan England but deadly anathema to Counter-Reformation Catholics and Calvinists alike, cannot be imagined by Albany and Kent on one side or Goneril, Regan and Edmund on the other. The one is committed to respect and unconditional obeisance to ancient authority, and the other to feel resentment and uncontrolled outrage at its abuses. And even if the French invasion temporarily yields odd allies and strange bedfellows, the basic issues makes the two parties irreconcilable. Here the Bard not only explains why some English Catholics would have welcomed the Spanish Armada, he also sees the Thirty Years War and English Civil War loom ahead; yet Shakespeare also tentatively hints how the deepest issues involved in these conflicts may have been solved.

So even if Albany's viewpoint would have been highlighted on Boxing Day 1606 when *King Lear* was first staged before James, there is no doubt that the alternative extreme could also have been emphasized in future productions and readings. The very fact that a cheap quarto edition of *King Lear* appeared in 1608, barely a year after that staging in James' court, suggests that the possibility of this other far more profane perspective than one pleasing to James was always lurking in the wings. Even if Regan or Goneril, like Luther during the Peasant's Revolt nearly a century before *King Lear,* did not want the "slaves" or rabble to replace the rulers, the seal of sanctity had been broken.

This is why Goneril, after deploring her husband's deference to Lear, also does not see anything wrong in flirting brazenly with Edmund. She probably knows Lear too well to have any illusions about his divine mandate to rule England, having seen far too much of the dragon in his rage. This is also why she seeks a husband who could better complement her own ambition and rage; Edmund, due to his own unloved upbringing, will be able literally to grasp who she really was and is. Her saying "our wishes on the way may prove effects," strongly suggests that Goneril had expressed to him her wish for such a consort; now that Albany has become even weaker and perversely irresolute, it seems as if his wife will "give the distaff into my husband's hands" and take over power herself.

It is with this intent that she bids farewell to Edmund by kissing him, giving him a token and pledging that he may expect "a mistress' commands" if he "dare venture" on his "own behalf." Then asking him to conceive her meaning, she suggestively says that her kiss, "if it durst speak, would stretch thy spirits up into the air" and finally promises him "the woman's services" due him that she cannot give "the fool," presumably Albany, who "usurps her body." Edmund's own, equally enigmatic, response, "yours in the ranks of death," reveals something of his dark nature to us. He is more focused single-mindedly on deadly revenge than power-hungry Goneril sees.

The ruling passions of Goneril, Albany and Edmund are ambition, reverence and death; while the first and last derive from revenge, Albany's reverence is based on nature and natural law. He accuses her of being more tiger than daughter and preaches that wisdom and goodness to the vile seem vile. His rebuke of Goneril echoes Lear's curse of sterility and predicts Edmund's necrophilia; he claims that a "nature that condemns its origin" (Lear) will "come to deadly use." It is why he fears that if the heavens do not intervene to save Lear, who is a priori "a father and gracious old man" to his eyes, "humanity must perforce prey on itself like monsters of the deep."

Yet even though Albany's prediction is correct, we must yet wonder if the prophet has placed his hands on the scales. Were it not for Kent's instigation of Cordelia's intervention, England would not have been plunged in war. Further, had Albany not been so irresolute before Lear's boisterous behavior, the matter could have been resolved domestically before the horrific events ending in Gloucester's blinding. As noted before, even Lear and Gloucester themselves saw that they had behaved badly and abused power. Far from being God's sacred anointed deputy, Lear was but a confused and angry old man who had forgotten how to love properly. While Albany sincerely believed, as Hobbes would, that mortals were too fractious and sinful to live together without a divinely ordained sovereign, a solution that suited his temperament quite nicely in that it gave him wealth, power and standing without ultimate responsibility, he could not imagine a commonwealth ordered in accord with and supportive of human equality. Albany also clearly sees women as naturally inferior; this is clear in the misogynistic language he uses on Goneril: "proper deformity seems not in the fiend so horrid as in women." In short, the devil's at least a gentleman gone wrong; and "however thou art a fiend, a woman's shape does shield thee," i.e., he is too much of a gentleman, or a coward, to treat his wife as her sex deserves. She in turn is disgusted at the pusillanimity he displays: "France spreads her banners in our noiseless land, with plumed helm, thy state begins to threat, whilst thou, a moral fool, sits still and cries, alack, why does he so?" His only response to this is to say, "See thyself, devil!" We must wonder whether he would have gone to war against the French had she not been there.

But now the chaotic situation is muddied further by news of Cornwall's death and Gloucester's blinding. While Albany sees this as evidence of justice sent from above, but laments the fate of Gloucester, Goneril sees that the situation could break both ways for her. On the one hand, it could bring her closer to rule over all England with Edmund. On the other, Regan, being already a widow, is better poised to make Edmund her spouse and destroy yet wedded Goneril's hopes. While Goneril exits to ponder the matter more, Albany hears that Edmund has betrayed Gloucester. This makes Albany pledge to reward Gloucester for his love for Lear, and to revenge his eyes. It seems that he too is blind in putting loyalty to old men before defense of his invaded country. We cannot forget that Gloucester will start a civil war to save Lear's life. We have not seen any grounds for supposing that Goneril or Regan intend to kill Lear. Gloucester is easily deceived; it is even possible that Edmund could have convinced his father of this in order to further incriminate him.

If we shift now to an allegorical/historical conceit where Lear is the pope or a papal God, Albany's stance permits a Marian restoration on formal grounds. By contrast, the sisters' responses to Gloucester's treason, "pluck out his eyes" and "hang him instantly," set up a theological choice between the death of God and a kind of Deism. In effect, Goneril's symbolically plucking out the eyes of God means a return to Elizabeth's stated policy of not allowing the eyes of God, "God's spies" as Lear later says to Cordelia, to look or "have windows into men's souls." God must not be weaponized.

Yet the next scene gives us a window into Cordelia's soul as well as providing welcome context regarding the French invasion. We first find that the French king, Cordelia's husband, has gone back home for some unforeseen but urgent reason. This establishes that the invasion was more than just a rescue mission, but it also shows that the English side was unlikely to have known of his return. We also see new evidence that Kent, while yet disguised, is the mastermind behind this whole operation; the gentleman's report of Cordelia's reception of his letters reveals that Kent is feeding her reports of how badly Lear is being treated by Goneril and Regan. And we have already seen how biased Kent is here. Mad or not, the king's person is sacred to him.

While her sorrow for Lear is genuine, Cordelia is also clearly pleased to see that he is estranged from her sisters; she is vindicated. This is why her tears and "happy smilets" are mixed, like rain and sunshine, one emotion not knowing how to deal with the other. Also, since this is the very gentleman we saw Kent send to her earlier, it can be concluded that some prior contact had been made with France, perhaps by Kent himself, before the story of the storm had been told. We do not know if the origins of this secret "French connection" were strategic or sentimental, but it could be surmised that with the tale of Lear's misuse by his older girls being a strong basis for a restoration headed by Cordelia rather than a French invasion of England, the departure of the French king now looks a strategic move, all the better to defeat united England this way.

Moreover, it also seems that Lear himself is now ashamed of what has transpired; Kent finds out that Cordelia heard all this before Lear was sent to Dover. Once the old king finds out what has resulted from reports of his ill-treatment, it could also be shame at his misbehavior before Goneril and Regan, since it brought on a French invasion, that keeps him away from the French. Cordelia knows that Lear is "as mad as the vexed sea" but yet she vainly persists in hoping to restore his "bereaved sense." She claims to be willing to do anything to bring this outcome about, while also knowing the root of this madness is not the accidental lack of repose that a doctor offers as an explanation; it is "ungoverned rage" from within Lear's soul that threatens to dissolve his life. This being so, there is little the "blessed secrets" of the earth can do for him.

Now hearing that "British forces" march towards them, Cordelia piously says, "O dear father, it is thy business that I go about." This weird and deliberate echo of Christ's words at the Temple must surely imply some equation or comparison of the two beloved children, son and daughter. We cannot know how ironic Shakespeare is being here, but for herself Cordelia protests that her arms are not incited by "blown ambition" but merely "love, dear love and *our aged father's right*" (Nalin's emphasis). But this means that, despite her claim that the French king only sent his forces due to her mourning and tears, she still plans to fight to restore a madman to the throne of England. If not, it would surely have been easy enough to send a smaller force to bear Lear off to France. It is thus not his life or sanity saintly Cordelia cares for; she is defending Lear's right to rule. Cordelia must view herself as a Messiah; she is doing her father's business and fighting for his kingdom. This amazing hubris, reminiscent of Queen Margaret's attempts to restore mad Henry VI to the throne, even at the cost of extending the Wars of the Roses, cannot be praised as filial piety.

Close analysis of its context points towards the probability that the patriarchal paradigm *King Lear* portrays is as powerful and poignant as it is perverse and provocatively flawed. We cannot but be appalled at the idea that a faithful daughter should be so doggedly devoted to her deposed but demented father that she would provoke and prosecute a war for his restoration to rule. Yet variations of this mad scenario have played out throughout recorded history. The power of this primal paradigm is such that its proponents, blinded to its poisonous properties, push aside probity. They try to resurrect what is rotten and repugnant, but their reactionary reverence refuses to let them recognize all that is rash, risky and reckless about this romantic rhetoric.

While we do not doubt that the devotion Cordelia feels for Lear is real, it must also be seen that this single-minded sincerity blinds her to many other factors that would otherwise warrant her close consideration. Only Lear truly exists in her sun-blinded reality; all other humans lack substance or intrinsic value. By deifying him she radically discounts the value of all other souls, especially those to be sacrificed in her war for his restoration. This, finally, is her deferred bid in Lear's perverse auction. She is willing to wage an unnecessary war to prove her love for him.

Meanwhile in strikingly exact contrast to their sister's worship of Lear, Goneril and Regan make Edmund the object of their competitive obsession. While Cordelia, Gloucester and Kent blindly worship the king, falsely endowing him with divine sanctity, the two sisters seem to be drawn to the bastard precisely because of his demonic cunning and devilish energy; they may also find relief in stripping off all false piety and speaking in the shameless idiom of commodity. Both forms of speech are perversions; the one too obsequious and the other too crass, but we can see how the latter offers relief from the compelled self-abasement of royal flattery. Yet just as common attraction to Edmund makes them alike, it also poisons their relation to each other; united once in their shared hatred of Lear, they are now divided by lust for Edmund. This is why, once Regan hears that Albany is in command of the Northern army, despite his wife Goneril being "the better soldier," a striking fact that is seemingly commonly known, her focus swiftly shifts to Edmund, asking her sister's trusted messenger Oswald if Edmund had speech with Albany, and wondering at the content of the urgent letter Goneril had sent to Lord Edmund.

Regan tells Oswald that Edmund was sent (by her) on a serious matter; it was "great ignorance, Gloucester's eyes being out, to let him live." As the presence of the old blind earl, like Arthur in *King John,* would "move all hearts against us," Lord Edmund is going "in pity of his misery" "to dispatch his nighted life" or deliver the *coup de grace* and moreover spy out the force of the enemy. It is worth noting here that it was Regan herself who originally wished to kill Gloucester, then told him gloatingly of Edmund's perfidy and finally sent him off blinded towards Dover. Edmund is entrusted with a truly villainous task; he is clearly expected to derive delight from this action. We may also note that the two brothers are both tasked to do the same thing. Edgar is asked by Gloucester to lead him to his death and Edmund is told by Regan to do the same deed directly. Most fortunately for both Edgar and Gloucester, the blinded old man is entrusted to his care.

Meanwhile Regan attempts to separate Oswald from Goneril's note. She tells him that it is better for Edmund to marry her: "My lord is dead— Edmund and I have talked, and more convenient is he for my hand." She urges Oswald to talk sense to Goneril. This cynical logic of commodity is common to them all; Edmund did not know that Regan had been widowed when he pledged himself to Goneril. The steward, as ambitious as Malvolio, must surely prefer the marriage of Regan to Edmund; he would be reinstated as Goneril's only confidante. Oswald also gladly accepts her offer of "preferment" should he kill the earl, his words, "would I could meet him, madam! I should show what party I do follow," show his soul. We are in a place where the sensible seem shamelessly wicked, and the well-intentioned are blindly devout and recklessly stupid. The *via media* between this pair of ugly extremes is entrusted to two hunted outlaws.

Now follows the famous Dover Beach scene where Edgar, as blind to the facts behind his sire's blinding as his father is bereft of sight, appears; he is guiding Gloucester to the high cliff from whence the earl intends to leap to his death. We must also infer that, in his *persona* as Poor Tom, Edgar is not in a position to interrogate his father about this decision. Indeed, he cannot even be expected to know that Gloucester intends suicide. And he must persist in his role for his own safety; Edgar knows that Gloucester yearns to see him but does not know that his sire has discovered his innocence—or at least deduced it from hearing of Edmund's perfidy. It can be seen why forgiveness may not be enough for Edgar; he could want his good name to be vindicated.

Edgar only knows that he is a "proclaimed" outlaw; indeed, he cannot even say for certain that it was Edmund who betrayed him. This is why he cannot discount Edmund's claim that Cornwall and Albany are both hostile to him. And it is clear that disgraced Gloucester cannot protect him if he were to resume his former identity. So, for both their sakes, he must remain as Mad Tom. The vexing matter of whether Edgar should reveal himself to Gloucester to dissuade him from killing himself or do so after he has prevented this suicide by other means remains unresolved. But clearly Edgar does need to find out more about the extraordinary events going on around him.

When he leads Gloucester to a plain as flat as a proverbial Dover sole, rather than the steep Dover cliff they were supposed to find, Edgar tries to convince his father that they are in fact ascending at a steep incline. The mythological backdrop to this scene is surely suggestive of the scene from Genesis where Abraham takes Isaac up a mountain to sacrifice him to God. But here everything is reversed: the land is flat, the son guides the father, it is the father who wishes to commit suicide and the son who must save him, and—most critically—the guilty father's atoning death is not demanded by an angry God. It is as if the sacred covenant of Father Abraham, the basis of the patriarchal order, is being reversed; and in due time, a mad God-King will arrive to confirm this reversal of the whole order of sin and guilt. And even more strikingly, before this weird apparition, a false prophet, whose name means God's will, will claim to have authority to kill the father; and yet it will be he (or his wicked message) who will duly be sacrificed instead.

Of course, the true cause of Gloucester's guilt, the sacrifice of one son at the behest of another, neatly reversing Abraham's sin of abandoning his illegitimate son for his heir, is ultimately quite illusory. Just as Ishmael did not die, and instead became the father of a mighty people, Edgar did not end up victimized by his father's blindness, but rather ends up redeeming Gloucester. Also, like Cordelia with Lear, he can forgive his father and, saying "no cause," write off the debt. If anything dies, it is the Old Testament Law and the old way of accounting by guilt and blood.

Edgar needs to perform a miracle to make his father overcome his despair and feel redeemed in a way that will allow him to live again. Though in truth a miracle is unnecessary because the result of original sin for which Gloucester feels so guilty, the loss of Edgar, never took place, his quite genuine experience of deep despair can only be erased by another equally compelling metaphysical event. Edgar might well ask, like Jesus: Is it easier to forgive your sin or to restore your son? Since the latter cannot be done yet, the former must suffice. This is accomplished by erasing the effects of Gloucester's "fall," even after the depths he plunges to are described vividly and the person who led him there is called a devil, although it was truly Poor Tom or Edgar himself.

It may thus be seen that two miracles occur. In the first place it seems that Gloucester is healed by divine mercy from a deed he was led to by a monstrous fiend, and yet it seems that the true miracle consisted in his being brought to his own exiled and disguised son and his then being guided by him. It is also the case that mankind itself is shown that the Fall was just an illusion. The conclusive proof of this powerful claim, for which Gloucester will see incontrovertible evidence later on, will occur when his beloved son Edgar is restored to his prodigal father. But even before this there will be a completely surreal divine encounter which will signify to us that the quite radical theological implications of the broader claim just made are well supported by the continuing action of *King Lear*.

Gloucester's attempt at suicide was in one sense merely an enactment of how "Pillicock sat on Pillicock Hill." Edgar, then speaking as Tom, reduces his sire's suicide to a charade so he may no longer blind himself of his responsibilities to the world but reenter it through sad gratitude and genuine speech. Or else, in self-pitying mode, he is as bad and lacking in self-knowledge as Lear, the original object of these lines. Gloucester must learn to stop seeing reality via Lear's eyes; we must hope that the blinded courtier will finally learn to see his sacred king as a selfish and mad despot and think instead of the sorrows Lear's entitled behavior has visited on other souls. It is also hoped that the earl will learn what Edgar learned by seeing him blind; the power to mourn about how bad things are for us only means our soul has yet to know the true depths of sorrow.

We might say that Gloucester sought to jump off a cliff because he could not stand to live at the bottom of a world turned upside down: he had lived most securely in a cosmos where nature is just and justice is natural, and that was all he needed to know. Edgar may also feel some bitterness at seeing that, while Gloucester had literally gone the extra mile for Lear, at grave risk to his own life, he did not make any real effort to let Edgar know he was sorry before trying to kill himself. In this respect, we find it striking that Gloucester cannot recognize his son's voice when Edgar lets his guard down. Gloucester was better at playing loyal courtier and lusty lover than at being a father. The tragic code allows that in "great affliction" a noble can save himself from shame after doing his best for his betters. As for Edgar, if he lives, "bless him": the blinded earl will not fight to cleanse his son's name.

Some of Tom's babblings hint that Edgar had played a dissolute courtier's life before Edmund inadvertently rescued him from this fate; now he must "trifle thus with his despair to save" his father from this abyss of self-pity. But while rough magic is needed to shake Gloucester from his obsolete view of England, Edgar fears that his sire's "conceit," or despairing desire to die, will be stronger than the unfallen nature which has saved him. This is why he must teach Gloucester the import of what has befallen him. As the father says "away and let me die" when approached by his son in a new rational persona, and even laments that one can no longer elude a "tyrant's rage" and "frustrate his proud will" (two qualities that unconsciously describe Lear) by death, he hears Edgar describe his escape from a terribly steep fall as a "miracle." Yet although Gloucester promises to bear affliction until it exhausts itself, the very gods now send another miracle before them. The spectacle of royal Lear, sometime anointed demigod to Gloucester's blind eyes, now revealing himself as a mad old fool to all our senses, not only reveals the ontological difference between king and god, it also exposes the vain folly of thinking the anthropomorphized jealous capricious storm god of the Old Testament, mimicked by Lear, to be a just representation of the truly divine. And even that god commanded not to use his name in vain or make images of him.

Lear's remarkable metamorphosis into a transgendered Ophelia seems to seal this prohibition. His mad words, "No, they cannot touch me for coining, I am the king himself," not only give ambiguous evidence to our point regarding images, they are followed by a lengthy, extensive and example-filled abrogation of the Old Law. Further, his uncannily deft refusal by deed to be caught, held, or even touched is the most literal embodiment possible of the Mosaic commandments against Davidic depiction. Edgar's words describing Lear as a "side-piercing sight" accurately suggest that we are seeing the tragic death of a god incarnate rather than a side-splitting comedy. And yet the two genres are united in the sight of the flower-decked Lear trying to raise an imaginary army. We must note that he appears just after Edgar falsely called Tom of Bedlam a fiend appearing as a man; we now find the supposedly sacred Lear to be but a delusional old man. Or better yet, his divinity is our delusion; Lear, for all his madness, is well aware that he "smells of mortality."

This duality persists when Lear, after suggesting that what he sees, however delusional, is truth, then concedes that he too is subject to nature. He does this by recognizing Gloucester, but calling him "Goneril with a white beard." Lear accuses the earl of being one of those flatterers who called him wise before he had even grown a beard. It was "bad divinity" to acquiesce to his every yes and no; the implication is that this unchecked indulgence led Lear to believe his will to be sovereign and divine. It took exposure to the wind and rain to reacquaint him with his humanity. This we recall is why he questioned Edgar, his philosopher, about the source of thunder. It is as if he thought a "reigning" king's rage caused thunder. He did not know himself as an effect rather than a cause. Yet in truth, Lear sees he is "no cause": "They told me I was everything; 'tis a lie. I am not ague proof."

When Gloucester finally identifies this mad voice ("is't not the King?"), Lear continues in this vein and replies, "Ay, every inch a king." It seems that he wishes to speak about the perversion of true justice but is swiftly diverted to arguing that lechery should be pardoned as natural ("Let copulation thrive"), to ranting against his daughters for their unkindness and sexual appetites. It seems that Lear attributes his abandonment by his daughters to their carnal desires. This would explain his odd words about "hot blooded France" taking Cordelia without a dowry, and also find cause for his rage that all three daughters left him to get married. Even his auctioning off of England to the child who loved him most is explained by Lear's perverse or jealous wish to be loved exclusively. Even in this equation of apostasy and whoring, Lear is like Israel's jealous god. We may recall that this deity also divided his land after the "infidelity" of the northern kingdom.

Lear then resumes talking of justice, which seems to be seen or felt better when one is blind as Gloucester. Reason is like "glass eyes" or eye-glasses: aiding only "to seem to see the things thou dost not," it corrupts feeling even as it makes sight of objects more acute. Reason cannot see origins, only things; it knows not that theft and justice are oft interchangeable. Rank, power and wealth license and hide great vices, even as they avidly punish petty flaws and minor failings in the lowly, weak and poor. But as his godson Edgar mourns this "reason in madness," Lear gifts him his vision. "If thou will weep my fortunes, take my eyes, I know thee well enough; thy name is Gloucester. Thou must be patient." These winged words, surely said to Edgar, are his gift. Lear will soon be found and forced back to the iron cage of regal necessity he tried to escape. He will be "the natural fool of fortune" again, but Edgar must never forget what Lear twice showed him.

As he senses his rescuers (or captors) stealthily approaching, Lear regresses back to insanity ("It were a delicate stratagem to shoe / A troop of horse with felt") and proposes using the same ruse to kill his sons-in-law. His mad six-fold repetition of the word "kill" shows us how Lear goes from uttering wise if impolitic general truths to obsessing over the deep wounds his ungrateful daughters have inflicted on his sick libido. This eternal recurrence between sanity and lunacy is surely the "wheel of fire" Lear will later say he's "bound to." But it yet remains possible for Edgar, or the reader, to separate wisdom from folly in his words. He no longer says anything sane and we never see his capture in *King Lear*. But Lear's last words as he runs off, with Cordelia's men in hot pursuit, are a hunting cry. It is as if, far from being the prey, he invites us to hunt his meaning.

Meanwhile, one of the gentlemen sent to find him, after calling Lear a sight far worse than what would be "most pitiful in the meanest wretch," says that Cordelia "redeems nature from the meanest curse which twain have brought her to." If this language reeks of Mariolatry even now, it would surely have seemed so in the paranoidly anti-Catholic atmosphere at the time of *King Lear*. In short, Lear's restoration would have to involve a combination of a foreign invasion like Philip II's Spanish Armada and a Counter-Reformation along the lines of what was infamously tried by his wife, Queen "Bloody" Mary, fifty years earlier. *King Lear* seems strongly opposed to any effort aimed at restoring absolute monarchy, especially one with a bit of theocracy thrown in.

But Edgar is still in the dark about what is going on. The various tableaus he has seen, each with a fair degree of absurdity or unreality, are all he has to go on. He does not yet know if Goneril and Regan are at war or allied against the French and Cordelia. Even more urgently, he has not heard how Gloucester came to lose his eyes and power. And lastly, there is the vexing matter of Edmund. He does not know what part his half-brother had in his downfall or Gloucester's.

Even as he assumes the not untruthful identity of a meek and sympathetic sufferer ("a most poor man, made tame to fortune's blows, who by the art of known and feeling sorrows, am pregnant to good pity") and is finally in a position to question his father, far more direct information miscarries serendipitously before him. Oswald arrives, sees Gloucester, and warns the "old unhappy traitor" his hour has come. Gloucester sadly replies, "put strength to it," but Edgar, now using a Somerset accent, defends his sire with his cudgel; he ignores Oswald's warning that "a bold peasant" must not protect "a published traitor," even after being called slave and menaced with death by the armed steward.

It soon proves that Edgar, though under-armed, is more than a match for Oswald's sword. As he dies the steward asks that the letter he carries be given to Edmund, Earl of Gloucester. Edgar opens a love letter written by Goneril reminding Edmund of their "reciprocal vows" and asking that he deliver her from the "loathed warmth" of Albany's bed by killing him. She signs it as one who wishes she were his wife.

But before he reads this letter, Edgar leaves to bury Oswald's body in the sand. His parting comment indicates that he is very much in sympathy with Albany, the "virtuous husband." He has earlier recognized Oswald as "a serviceable villain," well attuned in badness to serving the "vices" of his mistress. There is more than a whiff of misogyny in his claim to be amazed at "the undistinguished space of women's will"; although plotting murder is evil, this is surely no cause to issue such a sweeping condemnation of woman. Since Albany, as we have seen, is no saint, this shows another side to Edgar's character. Perhaps Nahum Tate was right in thinking him to be well suited to be priggish Cordelia's consort; she is her tainted nature's solitary boast. But neither of them can see that their whole way of morality is based on something that is now as baseless as the shifting sands of Dover Beach. Blind Gloucester sees this when, near the end of this scene, he soliloquizes that, as "the King is mad," he prefers to lose his own sanity and no longer know his "huge sorrows." He continues: "Better I were distract; / So should my thoughts be severed from my griefs." The God-King's madness makes patriarchal ethics based on order, trust and obedience bankrupt.

This is why, even as Act 4 ends with Cordelia in the company of Kent, paying fulsome tribute to his unmatched goodness, by which of course she means personal loyalty to Lear and herself, any real hope for a future restoration is compromised by the ailing Lear's mental and physical state. The best they can hope for, and this perhaps is what was sought originally, before Lear went rogue, is that Cordelia and Kent rule all England in Lear's name. And it also seems that Kent prefers to pull the strings secretly until the opportune time; until then, Lear's glorious memory and her unblemished name will make a cause to which all true Englishmen will rally.

However, even if Cordelia and Kent are sincere in their attachment to the sacred principles of monarchy, and here they would have to be like the Bourbons in neither learning nor forgetting anything, Lear's senility and mental volatility could overturn any hope of a nostalgic restoration. He is bent on revenge for the treatment he suffered at the hands of Goneril and Regan. But his two "bad" daughters, having gained power, are not likely to yield too easily or to grovel, and neither is his old man's love for Cordelia likely to be bound by any limit or measure. This means that the Restoration's future is doomed even if they win the battle. Thus, the hope Cordelia and Kent have in Lear must be quasi-religious, not based on practical things or moral ideas. Since a true king is divinely vested with power, he cannot turn human; that would lead to the kind of state Albany feared, one where humans would also devolve and fight like monsters of the deep.

Cordelia and Kent seem to believe that by treating Lear like a king again they will repair the "violent harms" done to his "reverence" by his daughters and resurrect Lear's true nature; by this logic, all have sinned by coming between the dragon and his wrath. Cordelia's unctuous tale of the awful sin of exposing Lear's venerable face to the storm already stands refuted by Lear's own words about his disregard of all the other poor wretches who endure much worse for far longer with no refuge; all Lear had to do was swallow his pride and ask to be let in. This is why we infer that her cause is not meant to be taken, in its stickily worded sentimentality, as just. It is truly absurd to plunge an entire nation into war just because a senile old man felt ill-treated.

When he revives, Lear is, as ever, a mixture of deep acuity and senility. He first and rightly says they did him wrong in taking him out of the grave. He is "bound upon a wheel of fire" so that his own tears scald like molted lead. While this wheel may just be Lear's recurring memory of the ingratitude shown him, the Homeric imagery hints that a sinner's own deeds plague him. Lear by this measure is suspended between his penitent soul and angry body. The very "abuse" and delusion he suffers is through not being allowed to atone for his sins. This abuse is paradoxically the work of those who flatter the king and do not let an "old and foolish" man pass away. Even when he asks Cordelia to pardon his terrible behavior, while yet unforgiving of her sisters, her famed answer "no cause, no cause" only feeds the dragon and retards his psychic rehabilitation.

While the mobile Kent/Caius hears that Edmund is in command of the forces of Cornwall, Kent himself is said to be in Germany with Edgar. This is a reminder that the fog of war persists; only we know the fate of Goneril's message to Edmund and Goneril is not aware that Regan probably knows of her desire for him. Both daughters eagerly await the return of ubiquitous Oswald with news from their beloved. We must also bear in mind that knowledge of motives is partial and speculative.

The only evident difference is in the language of the two factions. While Lear's side spoke in a sickeningly sentimental and sacramental idiom, those for England and the two daughters, while equally ruled by private agendas, are more doubtful of each other and speak in practical terms. It would seem that nobody, perhaps not even the duke himself, knows the mind of Albany. He seems to command his forces more out of mistrust of Goneril, "the better soldier," than from any firm conviction against Lear's cause. Like Hamlet, he too is conflicted between loyalty to the patriarchy and responsibility to the kingdom. Albany does not know what it is to be himself; ultimately mere resentment may prevail. Regan's snide quip that her "sister's man is certainly miscarried" adds to the sense that he is not man enough, least of all for Goneril; but there is also the implication of Oswald, literally Goneril's man, not carrying her message to Edmund.

Meanwhile Goneril, perhaps the most intelligent character in *King Lear,* is also acutely aware that her patriarchal and pusillanimous spouse is quite capable of making a deal with Lear and Cordelia at her expense. We have seen ample evidence of both his deep misogyny and seeming incapacity to believe that an anointed king could do wrong. This is another reason for Goneril's desperate love note to Edmund. Only the bastard has both the power of understanding the danger of her situation and the capacity to be of help. Regan is now a rival. Probably having been brought up starved of love, the sisters do not seem to be very close; only shared anger towards Lear and his favorite child brought them together. But now both need Edmund for equally valid reasons. It is a Hobbesian war of all against all; the effectual demise of the God-King has created a state of fear and only Edmund seems to have power sufficient or *virtù* appropriate for this new Age of Iron.

When Regan asks Edmund if he loves, or has gone to the forbidden or fork-ended place with her sister, he can claim with complete honesty to have only shown her "honored love" since he is capable of neither honor nor love. This is the main difference between Edmund and Lear's older daughters: they still desire love while he wishes to be desired but can really desire nothing but this desire, and is only truly ruled by the anti-desire to destroy all other forms of desire. And yet this total perversion of desire makes him something of an anti-Lear in that he hates all kinds of sentimental love, and is immune to the power of the sacred or the aura of ancient authority. Whether this unmoved mover is truly self-created and un-dependent on others, to the point of not having a soul in any true sense, yet remains to be revealed by events, but at least Edmund is decisive and ready to fight for England. To this extent he resembles the illustrious Bastard of *King John.*

By contrast, Albany, even after finally arriving with Goneril, continues to qualify their cause. The duke says he could not be valiant without being honest and then separates the French invasion, which he opposes to defend his land, from the "most just and heavy causes" or grievances of the king and others, which he cannot oppose. This is a clear sign that Albany is open to "redressing," whatever that means, the grievances of Lear's party should the English prevail in battle. To extend parallels drawn with *King John,* the duke is descended directly from Salisbury and Pembroke; even as they seem pious and scrupulous, the two never fail to find virtue beside their own best interest.

While Edmund's politic response is to flatter Albany, Regan bluntly asks the duke, "Why is this reasoned?" It takes Goneril to bite her tongue and stress the need to combine against their common enemy, pointedly observing that "domestic and particular broils" could be addressed later. Nevertheless, we see here both practical and selfish reasons for Edmund's later brutal actions towards Lear and Cordelia. Even if John's intended blinding of Arthur does not line up directly against Edmund's also rescinded plans for the royal father and daughter, especially as the one act caused an insurrection and the other followed it, we see how "reasons of state" in times of extreme crisis can appear to be as politically justified as they are morally repugnant. And even in strictly moral terms it is clear that Arthur's true angelic innocence is very different in quality from the deliberately irresponsible "saintliness" of Cordelia; Arthur tried to escape use as a figurehead while Cordelia deliberately provoked a civil war. Yet while his saintliness is real, her belated but melodramatic display of daughterly devotion is also staged to awe its audience.

We now return to our place in *King Lear* and see that despite the implicit compact that private broils had to be deferred, Regan's insistence that Edmund not be left alone with Goneril easily shows the latter that her widowed sister was anxious to keep her apart from the bastard. This it seems will also explain both Oswald's not coming back and the lack of a reply to her urgent appeal to Edmund for relief from Albany's misogyny and political weakness. But yet, despite solving this riddle, beleaguered Goneril does not refuse Regan's request that she join her in the tent. It thus seems that Albany's wife still puts the bigger political issue ahead of her personal predicament.

Meanwhile, in seeming consonance with this deferment of private issues until the French army is fought, Edgar appears in disguise to Albany. He asks the duke to open his letter before battle is joined, and also presumably, before he can take any action in connection with what he will learn. Edgar leaves promising that a champion will be at hand to prove the truth of what his letter says. It may be the case that Edgar's first responsibility is to protect old Gloucester from any harm, but he also points out to the duke that his information will be moot if the battle is lost. It also seems fitting that Edmund is hoist with his own petard. Just as he acted maliciously but not untruthfully in showing the fabricated letter to Gloucester, so does Edgar, the victim of Edmund's forgery, now repay the favor by giving to Albany the letter Goneril wrote Edmund. While Gloucester and Albany deserved to know their son/wife was unfaithful, there is still something wrong about how they were told.

We must bear in mind that Albany knows what is yet unbeknownst to Edgar, namely, that Edmund betrayed his father. The duke is likely to discount the bastard's plausible patriotic grounds for doing so. But this will not prevent the pusillanimous Albany from making full use of Edmund's intelligence and Goneril's generalship. Edgar's real concern could be that Edmund will try to kill Albany amidst the fog of war and seize the crown for Goneril and himself. This would doom and disgrace Gloucester and Edgar, who does not know how nihilistically negative and uncannily unerotic his half-brother's sentiments are. It is as if Edmund and Gloucester have independently come to the sad judgment: "ripeness is all."

Edmund himself has the last words before battle is joined. They reveal him to be both unerotic and by virtue of this absolute impotence also incapable of committing murder himself; as we recall, he only denounced Edgar and Gloucester, and did not carry out—for whatever reason—Goneril's urgent wish that he should kill Albany. Edmund seems to be most content as the third party in a frayed relationship he can control; the bastard knows that on his own he is nothing, He seems to be aware and fearful of this isolated condition. Having sworn his love to both sisters, each as jealous of the other as desirous of him, Edmund must see he is best beloved by remaining in this configuration. He does not feel especially drawn to either sister and could just as well be happy with neither. He also knows that "neither can be enjoyed if both remain alive."

Emulating his earlier assessment of the enemy forces which he diligently drew up but could not act on, Edmund's calculation of his erotic situation reveals that while Goneril would never stand for his taking widowed Regan, he could never have Goneril while Albany lived. We do not know if his impotence stems from a bastard's hatred of adultery or a personal inability to kill. Yet he is quite content to let the sister most desirous of him kill Albany after the duke's "countenance" has been used in battle. While it is hard to see why Regan would go out of her way to kill Albany for Edmund's sake, thus freeing her sister to marry him, it could be because the snobbish duke would not permit the promotion of an earl's bastard to equal ducal rank as Cornwall. Such an irrationally unselfish act would be the ultimate proof of Regan's unconditional love for Edmund. And the unspoken but logical following move would be for one of the sisters to kill her sibling.

Meanwhile, Edmund for his part would gladly rid the sisters, and England, of Lear and Cordelia. The rules of war allow punishment of their treason towards the realm and the pair stand for all that is most repugnant to his spirit of negation. And further, the restoration of Lear and regency of Cordelia would bring doom to her sisters, the speedy rehabilitation of loyal Gloucester and a scrutiny of the events that led to his blinding. Regan must have gleefully told cautious Edmund of how she added to the old earl's misery by revealing who betrayed him. As his own tenuous state demands that he "defend not debate," Edmund's first priority, if they win, is to dispose of Lear and Cordelia. If his side loses, as with Edgar, the matter is moot for legitimacy has won. Only if the old law is defeated can the victors try to create a better order to replace once sacred kings and dated ways. But the new rulers' own souls may stealthily evade being studied.

The battle itself passes undescribed. While it takes place we merely see Edgar take Gloucester to safety under the shade of a tree. Leaving his father there and asking him to pray "that the right may thrive," Edgar leaves promising to bring comfort should he ever return. Nothing is said of the nature of his business. Since Edgar has yet to identify himself, he has taken the risk of leaving his father without the knowledge that one of his sons left him to fight the other. It seems callous that he leaves his heartbroken father without any sort of reconciliation, but the disgraced heir is resolved to vindicate himself against Edmund before returning to Gloucester as Edgar. Perhaps he would not seem to deceive a blind man or disappoint him further until their wrongs are righted and his father need no longer be guilty for his fall to the level of Poor Tom.

Yet when the news comes of Lear's defeat, Edgar hurries back to take his father away, with no care for the risk to his honor. When Gloucester refuses, arguing that a man may rot anywhere, Edgar replies by rebuking these "ill thoughts" and telling him that all men must endure change, "their going hence even as their coming hither." When the disguised son reminds his blind father that "ripeness is all," echoing Hamlet's "readiness is all," and urges Gloucester to come on, the old man accepts the truth of his words. We cannot choose to stop learning from life. This turn from "rotting away" to "ripeness" rejects Edmund's nihilism and the soulless sanctity of Lear's side. We must always hold ourselves ready to consummate life by being open to more spiritual growth, gladly "learning and teaching" as Chaucer said, and gifting ourselves to the world in this fulfilled condition. This ripeness is an apt Renaissance response to Aristotle's static teleology; it makes our gods and ourselves ready to celebrate what is genuinely divine about the cosmos. As we saw, Lear and Gloucester gained deep wisdom at their worst moments in late life; but only a truly high culture can go past playing with power and use the fullest insights of its richest souls.

But there is also a more specific way in which Gloucester and Edgar, two disgraced men are both ripe: they still have confessions to make before they die. While Edgar realizes that his father and he must be reconciled before he tries to have it out with Edmund, Gloucester must also feel obliged to tell others of how foolishly he had treated his two sons. So much of what is tragic in *King Lear* comes from an inherited human inability to settle debts of this kind, to offer a logos or account, at the *Kairos* or right time, when the time is ripe.

Like festered lilies that smell worse than weeds, accounts not settled in a timely way turn into interest bearing bad debts or sins, laws or letters that kill, angry ghosts, or deadly dogmas that spread despair and division far and wide. But just as all the Bard's characters are ripe in being unique and individuated, so too must we see their God. *King Lear* shows how the old king must die along with the old idea of god; their shared traits of power, jealousy and anger are superseded by human virtues. This is why *King Lear's* end may also be more ripe than tragic; it is tragic to hoard raw power in one man, when its true use or ripeness is in liberality toward many souls. Only "loving" god, and so finding it sinful to love the world or other men, may be the worst sin of all.

The long final scene of *King Lear* begins with victorious Edmund giving orders for Lear and Cordelia to be taken away until the proper authorities decide their final fate. At this Cordelia piously boasts that they "are not the first, who with best meaning have incurred the worst." It is striking that, even at this point, she has no remorse for waging unnecessary war out of love for a senile king; there is no doubt that she views Lear as a god who is owed unconditional worship and fealty. It is in this very spirit that religious fanatics in the play's time and ours have waged endless wars; we cannot avoid the recognition that the attributes of this jealous angry deity demand no less. And it is even more ironic that Cordelia waged war in Lear's name despite his own wishes; he would far prefer to spend the final senile days and months of his life in her exclusive company. His doting wish is for them to spend their time continually blessing and forgiving each other.

Cordelia even goes on to say that were it not for her love for her father, she could be stoic and "outfrown false Fortune's frown"; instead, now, she is "cast down." This must also imply that she has been abandoned by her husband as well. There is no talk of her ransom or return to France. It could be that the king of France feels just as used as poor Octavia was by Marc Antony. The near parallel paths followed by *King Lear* and *Antony and Cleopatra*, two plays written at the same time, is our key to decoding the different answers these two tragedies give in response to very similar questions; neither Antony nor Cordelia can ever truly separate themselves from Cleopatra and Lear. Even Cleopatra's name means what Cordelia represents: her father's glory. The bond is too strong.

Cordelia is also anti-Christian in that she is incapable of exogamous love; she is her doting sire's messiah or warlord. Unlike Jesus, who will not wage war, not even for his chosen people, she will fight her country for her father. Lear himself is a Shylock-like, non-Trinitarian Old Testament God, jealously obsessed with ducats/dukes and daughters, but lacking a true logos or son. His three daughters stand for King Lear's most essential attributes: pride, rage, and jealous desire. There is more proof that Lear is a non-Trinitarian deity in that the love of this jealous Father and his silent loving Child does not produce a Spirit that goes past them, to the land and the world; in this sense it is correct to say that *King Lear* is set in a pre-Christian Britain. If King Lear had his way, Cordelia and he would be worshipped like a God and his co-redeeming Blessed Virgin Daughter.

From England's standpoint Edmund is much like *King John*'s Bastard; he has fought for the land and is absolutely justified and patriotic in taking preemptive steps against Lear being restored to the throne. Any king who places his personal interests above those of the very country that he has sworn to protect can be said to have abdicated by this act; thus, his name neither can nor should be used by others to advance their own agendas—be they stupid, sentimental, or simply selfish. As Lear saw in his moments of vision, a true king must serve the common good; any ruler who does not is an oligarch.

But while Edmund's next step, of secretly ordering the execution of Cordelia, makes him seem more like King John than the Bastard, here too, as in the case of that first Brexit, the real move is made against the God-King. In short, just as John is really fighting the pope, with Arthur being Pope Innocent's anointed and disposable pawn, Edmund could be said to have been opposing an entirely corrupt and self-serving system based on placing the senile, the sacramental and the stagnant status quo before the state itself. He is like Machiavelli: ruthless but not unpatriotic. Even if he is not unselfish, this selfishness is not at variance with the best interests of England. In other plays, Shakespeare has skillfully shown us how a villain can be disguised as a hero; in *King Lear* by contrast, we see how an antihero with dirty hands can be made to seem a villain *tout court*.

By its elevation of a man as a God-King, royal absolutism denies the dignity, freedom and very humanity of all other human beings. To this virtually exceptionless extent, it is a kind of back-door nihilism, as foolish as it is dangerous. Indeed, we can see how, in their leading men to justify the death of many millions of fellow Christians, all in the same God's name, over the Thirty Years War which began scarcely a decade after *King Lear,* vain doctrines of royal and or papal absolutism, whether fighting for or against a jealous God's rights, end up doing only the devil's business. Shakespeare must have been well aware of this possibility; the wicked St. Bartholomew's Day Massacre of 1572 was just one example of the kind of murderous orgy that could be planned and promulgated by princes, performed by pious peasants in God's name, and later even be praised by the pope himself. But if a conscience, or even objective awareness of an evil act may be overridden by a divine mandate, in a way that deems it sinful not to do a clearly criminal deed like a genocide or massacre, then there is something wrong with the party defining such an evil action as God's command. More often than not this has far more to do with the personal interests of their leader, or the "sacred" institution he is bound to, than God's true will. It is in these cases that a bastard's clear eyes, incredulous skepticism, and unclouded mind are useful.

This is why a bastard must never aspire to replace those whose crimes he exposes; by becoming part of any sacred institution exempt from moral criticism, we only deny ourselves the very self-knowledge or Socratic ignorance that made our own disinterested insights originally possible. Rulers must neither make windows into men's souls, nor claim the right to demand violent acts, before humbly explaining the harsh contexts requiring such deeds. We cannot let dead old men impose dogmas making some better than others by boon, blood or birth-order; arbitrary whims of gods, kings, and fathers cannot make other lesser men into sinners, strangers, and bastards.

All claims to have direct access to the divine, especially those that give the prophet privileged status above all others, must be treated with extreme prejudice; as Gloucester discovered, the moral terrain traversed by all humans is as fair, flat and finite as Dover Beach. The gods play us hard but true and the only true abyss exists within the soul. We must recall the lesson of Greek mythology that the last man to dine with the gods, Tantalus, proudly fed them his own children; the moral is that we destroy each other, even those we try to love, if we try to love the gods or "game" the cosmos. These rules may help us to find the import of *King Lear's* last scene and *King Lear* itself.

When defeated Cordelia, madder than her father at this point, wishes to see "these daughters and these sisters," Lear tried to warn her he had "no cause" but she could not hear him. At the end, his sole concern was for his beloved daughter, the "poor fool" with whom he would preside over infinite space in a nuthouse. Yet, ironically, Edmund's order to kill Cordelia gives these two sirens of Dover Beach infinite time to entice histrionic actors to fall in love with them or, even worse, to misguide true believers in sacramental sovereignty. *King Lear's* end shows that old Lear, like Hamlet's ghost, can still skip and kill with "his good biting falchion"; as with assassinated Caesar, the symbol is more potent dead than alive, and its evil outlives *King Lear's* sane message. And, saddest of all, Lear's late insights into kingship, like Julius Caesar's plans for Rome, lie buried in the sand.

Perhaps another reason for this failure of the lessons of *King Lear* to be seen rightly is the fact that all the play's surviving characters are morally exhausted. Asked to "speak what we feel" we find we cannot do so by the time this tragedy ends. In this respect *King Lear* fittingly but sadly resembles *Hamlet*, the very work it continues, clarifies, and consummates. By study of these fathers and children in *King Lear* we find that the worst vices of the older generation are often shared or inherited unevenly; humans are not created and individuated by the distant yet just gods or by our stars. We are formed and forged by the damage all souls inherit and suffer as we selfishly struggle to seek love in a wounded world. Only by viewing the ending of *King Lear* in this way will it make sense.

The play's endgame sees various paired souls eliminate each other. Yet at its conclusion those that remain on the boards are hardly fitted to continue the story they have been asked to give posterity. One of these two principals, Albany, reveals his snobbish pusillanimity when he refuses to let Edmund, who has just won the battle, remain in possession of Lear and Cordelia. Even as he has just given orders for the two to be disposed of, Edmund still gives sensible grounds for their being held under guard, pointing out that while Lear's age and title could still sway some of the common people, others who yet sweat, bleed or mourn lost friends could react very differently. We also note that while the duke had justified the rebels who sided with the French ("most just and heavy causes make oppose"), he cannot feel for men who patriotically fought for England.

Yet Albany responds, just as Henry IV did to Hotspur in a similar context, by demanding custody of the prisoners. This could very well have to do with his own shaky position; he holds power by a wife whom he knows to hate him as much as he does her. Only control of the king gives him legitimacy in his own right; by this logic, Albany wishes to rule England as Lear's regent. And there is also the matter of the letter he was handed by disguised Edgar. Even if the duke was not inclined to believe that Edmund actively supported Goneril's plotting against him, snobbish Albany will be cautious about entrusting too much power to one he knows to be of low birth, disloyal to his father, and openly hostile to Lear. All three counts prejudice him against Edmund.

Edgar's challenge fortuitously gives Albany a way of hitting Edmund where he is weakest. All can see that "Gloucester" has behaved valiantly in the battle and seems favored by fortune. He is also well beloved by both of Lear's legal heiresses; it is only over his treatment of Gloucester that

Edmund may yet be foiled from supplanting Albany and becoming *de facto* ruler of Britain. And since all that Edmund did in this case confirms admirably to the principle of placing country before his treasonous father, only his voluntary decision to accept a challenge to his filial honor, coupled with exposure of his seeming double-dealing with Goneril and Regan, makes it possible for cowardly Albany to play the two sisters off against each other and foil all three of his rivals.

As suggested earlier, it would seem that Edmund, Goneril and Regan are all moved by Thanatos rather than Eros; the sisters seem to hate each other and Lear even more than their professed love for Edmund, and "Gloucester" himself seems more driven to expose and exploit corruption than to actually enjoy the spoils of victory himself. There is something whimsical about Edmund choosing to accept the unknown knight's challenge rather than questioning Albany's completely specious argument against Regan's conferring all her powers on him. It was in a like spirit that Hamlet chose to fight Laertes instead of disclosing Claudius' damning letter to the Danish court. Both seemed to feel that readiness is all; their last deeds are marked by this spirit of ripeness.

Before turning to the duel between the brothers, we must note that Albany did not suspect that Edmund had already given orders for Cordelia to be killed. Had this been so, the cowardly duke might well have given up the game as lost. And neither did Goneril: otherwise, she would not have succumbed to despair and killed herself after having successfully dispatched her sister.

Edmund's order that a cord or rope be used to fake Cordelia's suicide by hanging hints again how our own vices, in this case the cord tying her to Lear, destroy us. And her death is enough to drive mad Lear back over the edge. But just as Edmund is unable to give the *coup de grâce* directly himself, we must also see that Albany is incapable of fighting "Gloucester," even after having brazenly accused him of treason. This is why it was lucky for Albany that Edgar could act as his champion; Albany could not refuse to fight a half-breed bastard himself without incurring the prompt accusation of cowardice. And it may well have been Edgar's extremely pointed words of challenge that compel Edmund to fight "an unknown opposite," as Goneril put it. Edmund is still guilty enough for his acts towards Gloucester and Edgar to silence these "hell-hated" charges speedily. He has no cause to feel guilty of treason toward the realm. Like a philosopher, his task is to rid the land of old sanctified lies and open men's souls to the nothing. Time is open again.

While the outcome of the duel is predictable, and also sets us up for the unexpected ending of *King Lear*, we may also note that Edmund's peculiar mix of personal guilt and long-term indifference, tied with Edgar's desperation, may have led to his defeat. Like his father and brother, he too seems to feel that "ripeness is all." But this brings Goneril to the brink of despair as she sees her champion and protector against Albany go down. After having poisoned her rival for his hand, she expected Edmund to prevail and vindicate her cause against the duke. She saw after he fell that the duel was a setup. Goneril is Queen in her own right and above the law. But her hopes of fighting against Albany diminish when he produces her letter to Edmund. This parallels the way King James' mother, Mary Queen of Scots, met her end. The incendiary tone of the letters both queens wrote, spiced with hints of unchastity, led to Mary's deposition flight to England.

But we wonder if Goneril's suicide is as contrived as Cordelia's; while Albany sends an officer to "govern" his "desperate" wife, a gentleman with a bloody knife arrives conveniently to recount her confession and death. This use of a *deus ex machina* hints that Goneril is to Lady Macbeth what Albany is to her husband, Macbeth; but it also follows that while she is more homicidal than suicidal, the duke is more like Edmund than may seem. The dying God-King has no son, and *King Lear* is clearly not a Christian play in this sense, but his son-in-law Albany is like *Measure for Measure's* creepy Vincentio, the "Duke of Dark Corners," in that, while seeming gentle, pious and good, he is far more complex, corrupt and self-serving than his sanctimonious speech suggests. And while King James is much like both dukes Vincentio and Albany, he was also very pleased to be hailed by the title of a notable figure in our last play, *Antony and Cleopatra*: Augustus. But analysis of this complex and consequential person, the adopted son of god, must be deferred until then.

CHAPTER FIVE
ANTONY AND CLEOPATRA
AND THE UNARMING OF EROS

Antony and Cleopatra traces Caesar's legacy, which was divided like Gaul between the men he favored most: Brutus, Octavius and Antony. Sphinx-like *Julius Caesar* asks us what Caesar and Rome truly were, even as we are urged to prioritize Caesar's qualities. While Brutus most values honor, this virtue dies with his suicide. As for Caesar's ambition, the very quality for which he was killed by Brutus, it surely transfers to his legal heir: Octavius. But Caesar's heart, his rare synthesis of clemency and concupiscence, passed to Antony. It is Antony who accuses Brutus of breaking Caesar's heart. It is only Antony—who cuts off his oration over Julius' body because his heart is in the coffin with Caesar—who knows and partially embodies classic Eros. But this immortal longing leads him, tragically, to Cleopatra. If classical culture began with Patroclus' sacrifice, it ends with Cleopatra's suicide. But while I will study the Bard's poignant depiction of the death of Tragedy, noting Augustus' resurrection of Hamlet as strong-armed Fortinbras, while Antony's faithful slave Eros is asked by him to unarm and slay his master, I look past these sad events, to a cosmic order that vindicates Antony and Cleopatra.

Antony's most prophetic words, "The evil that men do lives after them, the good is oft interred with their bones," will help us interpret the action of *Antony and Cleopatra*. Even as Brutus vainly addressed the Roman populace as "lovers," he worshipped honor to the extent of denouncing as "ambitious" those like Caesar who championed the needs of the plebs against the privileges of his own old-blooded class. And while erotic Antony lacked the ambition to take on the cold-blooded "will to power" of Octavius, the latter inherited this, Caesar's least agreeable quality, increasing it blindly and furiously, while uprooting republican honor and mutilating love. Eros, the quality Julius Caesar would have inherited from his ancestor Venus, is reduced to the oligarchic and anti-political proportions of family love, patriarchal power and property values. The ugly import today of this proto-Freudian move from Caesar's clemency and Christian charity, both erotic and "other-oriented" virtues, to thumotic self and familial assertion is all too clear. It is against this backdrop that we see how Augustus' Rome (and its corporate logic of power and empire) subverted, absorbed and defeated Jesus and the integrity of the early Christian church.

It is vital that readers of this play should bear in mind that Shakespeare is writing at a time between two eras, after the Renaissance and Reformation, and before the fast approaching Puritan and Presbyterian age which will plunge England into ruinous religious war and civil chaos. Shakespeare's was the first English generation that read the Bible in its vernacular. This could have led him to defend Christian humanism and true charity against a three-headed threat: the old Church's blind ossified corruption, the wily but uneasy Machiavellian statecraft of his own time, and the fanatical fundamentalism of the future. Even though a complete account of this far-reaching claim is impossible within my current limits, *Antony and Cleopatra* seems to point this reader in that direction. The parallels between the *realpolitik* that allows Octavius to defeat the unarmed eros of Antony and Cleopatra in their day, the panicked paranoia of the Bard's time, and the inexorably dehumanizing will to power in our own, are too plain to deny once we see how this play, like so many others, first seduces us into sharing a villain's vision; we cannot forgot how Shakespeare led us to secretly sympathize with, or even applaud, the evil machinations of Richard III, the self-serving wars of Henry V or even the solipsistic madness of Hamlet. We thus simultaneously see both *how* tragic virtue is defeated through slander in the public eye, and also why, bought, betrayed and buried, it can yet make future generations rally to a fallen flag. Even if Caesar's cause pleases the gods, the conquered cause pleases Cato.

Antony and Cleopatra begins by setting us up to see the lovers through censorious Roman eyes. Can we bypass Caesar's propaganda? *Antony and Cleopatra*'s first speaker, Philo, who only speaks in Act I scene I, roundly denounces the sad spectacle of Antony, the triple pillar of the world, a man once compared to Mars or Hercules, turned into a crippled Vulcan: "the bellows and the fan to cool a gypsy's lust." He said "I would prefer not" to the very basis of Roman thought and deed, the Virgilian and proto-Hobbesian imperative "to spare the conquered and battle down the proud" that made the relentless rule, rape and ruin of the whole world the manifest destiny of a little Italian city. Although *Antony and Cleopatra* is set well before the life and death of Jesus, many references to Cleopatra's rival, "Herod of Jewry," remind us that Rome was fully on the side of the hated oppressor of the Jews.

Rome is ruled by Mars. Hated Greek Ares has been fully rehabilitated and loved devotedly by the city on the Tiber. While Caesar only wages ceaseless war for the pious end of universal peace, Antony's refusal to fight for Rome's greater glory is ignoble since the triumvir's violent virility is arrested by a Circe-like witch; even his noble wife wages wars in his name, albeit against Octavius. Yet we soon find that any good Roman marriage has little to do with love; it is entered into for political and economic reasons. This is why Caesar and Antony agree to patch up their differences by a conjugal alliance; following his wife's death, they become brothers by Antony marrying Caesar's just widowed and still pregnant sister, Octavia. But while this makes sense in Rome, none of Antony's men believe that he will stay away from Cleopatra; while Octavia is but a perfectly demure Roman matron (they may never have consummated their marriage if we are to lip-read), Egypt's last queen is divinely fascinating: "neither age can wither nor custom stale her infinite variety." The mad Roman obsession with endless war is rivalled by the limitless erotic powers of Cleopatra. Eros is as sacred to Antony, Cleopatra and Egypt, as Mars is to Caesar, Rome and its Empire. But, as the foolishly frank clown tells Cleopatra, Eros is but an armless worm (phallus) in Rome's empire; here fertility and family trump freedom or fraternity.

The break between the two brothers (in law), thus killing the Republic and founding the empire (consuls rule jointly) was Caesar's work. Like Romulus (or Cain), he slays his brother and builds a city. Following the causality of the play, it is Octavius who "wages new wars against Pompey" with whom the triumvirs had just become reconciled, and then deposes Lepidus, on a flimsy pretext. Both weighty actions were performed without Antony's assent. It is only then that Octavia goes to Rome, still hoping for a reconciliation, and Antony returns to Cleopatra. Even here, it could be said that, Caesar having broken their pact and refused him troops, it was necessary for Antony to seek an alliance with Egypt, if only to fight Parthia. But it is very easy now for Caesar to resume Hamlet's role, as heaven's scourge, with Antony as the scapegoat.

It is Caesar, the self-effacing master of propaganda, who takes the gravest offense at his sister's inconspicuous arrival at Rome and makes it a *casus belli*. He gives full credence to reports that Antony and Cleopatra have set up their own alternative empire in defiance of the *Pax Romana*, and cannot countenance any defiance of his ultimate authority over the whole Roman world. The easy adroitness with which the play takes outraged Octavius' grievance at face value dares the careful reader to see that defiantly independent Elizabethan England, and its erotic Virgin Queen herself, would have been seen the same way by Catholic Europe and the Roman Church. While James I, a self-righteous misogynist, who yet saw himself as a peacemaker, avenger and unifier of kingdoms, saw himself as Augustus and would have deplored Elizabeth/Cleopatra's coquettishly cunning conduct, many in court would have felt nostalgia at this characterization. Despite her foibles, Cleopatra inspired devotion, embodying tragic beauty in a way that none but Helen had before, and brought out the best in those around her. But like Trojan Helen, or Elizabeth, we must concede that the human signifier often fell short of what it represented.

Further, returning to our play, we may also see that this sublime power, like Socrates' maieutic skill or Jesus' gospel, could also make those coming under her rare erotic influence unwilling to play the ugly games the time demanded of them. This could partially explain Antony's conduct at Actium. Hamstrung by treachery and trickery, he loses the stomach for a bloody battle that would pit Roman against Roman and continue the carnage of the Civil War. Also, in making Cleopatra, *qua* Venus, his soul's focus, this incarnation of Hercules is forced to follow the flight of a fearful queen—away from the epic sea battle and down from their high imperial pinnacle.

Yet it is at this point, at the nadir of the lovers' fortunes, that the tragic beauty of *Antony and Cleopatra* finally comes into sharp focus. Even as Octavius cynically schemes to have Cleopatra betray Antony as a condition of her forgiveness, thus emulating her brother's slaying of Pompey, and more of Antony's men desert him to follow Caesar's ascendant star, the doomed queen robs the victor of his triumph by elevating Antony and herself to a transcendent realm that a Roman Emperor could never attain: "No grave on earth shall clip in it a pair so famous," Caesar himself admits.

We see through all of his frantic negotiations with Cleopatra, both before and after Antony's death, that Octavius needed Antony to be killed by Cleopatra before she submitted to him and became part of his triumph. In this way only could he lay claim to the entirety of Julius Caesar's spirit. Octavius' wars were only against Cleopatra; he could not be seen to kill Caesar's avenger. Instead, both Brutus' honor and Antony's love, essential qualities of Caesar, were found to be distinct from his infinite ambition. His total victory at Caesar's funeral games will so be forever tainted by the absence of Antony and Cleopatra to testify to the honorable and generous way he wrested absolute power. His triumph now means no more or less than the end of history; it merely marks a time when there is nothing beautiful left on this earth to incur the gods' envy.

Octavius Caesar's victory represents the utmost consolidation of one-man rule over the whole Mediterranean world. This ambition was the least attractive of divine Julius' attributes. Thus, did Cassius' bitter words to Brutus turn prophetic truth, however replete with irony the events by which they were fulfilled turned out to be. Was it not in the Babylonian peace imposed by Caesar Augustus that Christianity entered the world? But could this ugly *ananke*, the necessity which deems that republican politics become a war of all against all, and end in autocracy, have been averted by means less draconian that those Octavius or Constantine used? In short, does Christianity have to accept Paul's claim in *Romans* that all power comes from God? Must this mean that the Christian Church, once an *Ekklesia* or assembly of Jesus' loving followers, has to become a corrupt clerical cadre, constantly trying to control, consolidate and centralize power? It is possible to argue that *Antony and Cleopatra* points us towards a less monolithic metaphysic, very compatible with Jesus' teachings and also less prone to being hijacked by a blindly imperious will to power.

Octavius' triumph is surely comic, for the Republic now passes to "a universal landlord." Yet the absence of distinction, for all strive for the same utilitarian uniformity and even Augustus wears robes woven by his virtuous wife, is surely to be lamented. Speech is effectively abolished; the Emperor will address the senate and people of Rome and they will obey his imperative voice. Like Augustine's God, he knows them better than they know themselves. While appearances are preserved, they mean nothing. In this thrifty proto-Hobbesian epoch, a commodious life is lived in the suburbs, and the only human tasks will be family fertility, trade and defensive war. Though Antony was denied the life of a private citizen, now every ex-citizen can be a last man at the end of history. The hope is that politics, and perhaps the soul itself, will wither away; both are redundant in an age presided over by a ruler called the Son of God. But this paranoid consolidation of power must justify itself. It can only do so by seducing a monotheistic religion to its ends. It is justified by the dogma of original sin. After this the Dark Ages had to follow.

What is the tragic alternative to this "comic" end to classical history? Are Antony and Cleopatra more than dissolute pagan archetypes, as splendid as they were short-lived and sinful? If there is an alternative to imperial Rome, an authoritarian state where all outlaws must meekly submit to slavery, it must give a better, more fulfilled, account of the soul and happiness. In short, the continual Roman pursuit of power, a restless diseased state Augustine saw as original sin, which must be punished by political coercion, finds its telos in a civilized Hellenized life. This was why Antony asked to live as a private citizen in Athens after Actium. Rome was too much under the sway of money and militarism for him to find joy there. But even if he lost Cleopatra, he still had memory of the beauty she brought to his life; it was perhaps this experience of flourishing in Egypt that ended his Herculean pursuit of pleasure and dulled his appetite for endless battle. Antony, who once fed the mob flesh, learned to cook raw power and savor lasting happiness.

What of Cleopatra? It is she after all who is queen of tragic space and divine epiphany. How will she staunch the terrible wound of human existence? Can her beauty save the world, teach us to say "stay, thou art so fair," and arrest the terrible energy of the will to power? Though Antony's suicide is more pathetic than noble, Cleopatra's death-scene is sublime tragedy; but she knows that the spectacle is only completed by sharing the immortal scene with, and so redeeming, Antony. He may be seen through her eyes only. By refusing to let their dead bodies be shown in Rome, their love is saved to mystify the world, inspire us, and even confound envious Caesar.

While empire and centralized imperial religion seek to reduce chaos, but end up stifling the soul and reducing all to uniform units and eunuchs, great art reminds us that the line dividing good from evil (and nobility from slavishness) runs through every human being. Cleopatra, the last of the tragic Greeks, is Shakespeare's masterpiece. Her power to bring out the best and worst in us is seen in her maids' devotion, Rome's hate and Antony's love. Was Cleopatra's once scheming and sybaritic life enlivened by Antony's great energy and generous heart? Did he play Orlando to her Rosalind? This is why her lament for him rings true. They made each other more beautiful and their love threatened to overflow in the world. They were equals in a way Cleopatra could never be with the divine Julius. If Antony jealously feared that "riggish" Cleopatra would betray herself trying to charm priggish Octavius, her suicide, unruled by false guilt, proves her ultimate integrity and deep love of Antony. The doomed queen's cosmic vision of her lover, bringing the world light, and surpassing all in liberality as he stands uniting heaven and earth, is of a Julius Caesar with the soul of Christ. It stands in contrast to Cassius' prophetic idea of a Caesar who straddles the world as a Colossus. "Past the size of dreaming," this ideal Antony makes Octavius look too much like lean hungry Cassius. Caesar's suspicious nephew misreads men too much. As a result of his Hobbesian squint, this king of infinite space denies the soul and kills the polis.

Antony and Cleopatra seems to teach that filial fury and righteous rage blind the eye and misdirect the soul; these counterfeit virtues make us fearful and self-forgetful. By contrast, eros allows every soul to be seen in its unique power to give to the common good and find true joy in a healthy polis. While angry thumos endlessly reifies psychic entities, eros and beauty unmakes its works and lets the event of no-thing-ing occur. Only by soul and polis is the cosmos seen in its beauty.

Tragedy triumphs in its acceptance of vulnerability. It trusts that what's unique and best about the soul will survive its chronic temptation to deny itself and just settle for banal survival. Right from her first lines in the play, Cleopatra is well aware that the lovers' mortal flaws would be maligned in Rome and slandered for all posterity. But she also sees that Caesar is not happy: "Not being Fortune, he's but Fortune's knave." His joy is not from his own soul, from bringing out the best in others; he prefers fear over love and being envied over being vulnerable. After killing Antony, his Don Giovanni, Octavius, by the end of a long life will turn Rome into a marble mausoleum, a Hades populated by angry ghosts and dead laws that hold the living hostage. The penultimate action of the play, the doomed queen and her maids literally hauling dying Antony to higher ground, illustrates tragedy's response to this soul-killing evil. Just as beauty saves the world, truly human life is sustained by a transcendent cosmic order that gives the grace to live nobly and die well. This is why we must renounce raw power and forsake its perverse pleasure. Only in love's fire is a soul's potential "cooked" and offered to gods and men. This is *Eudaimonia*.

I end by claiming that Shakespeare's prophetic power rings true in three distinct eras: the age setting the story, his day, and even our own time. While he allows the surface of *Antony and Cleopatra* to follow the official version of the tale, keeping close to Plutarch, these "Roman thoughts" are quite gainsaid by the beauty of the words he uses to depict Cleopatra, Antony and their love. Although we still live in a world ruled by power, property and paranoia, *Antony and Cleopatra* reminds us that the West's erotic origins, Greek genius and the Gospels, can yet redeem the soul from imperial and/or corporate structures that interpose stultifying laws and stale traditions between it and the truly divine. A soul can be inspired to swim, Dolphin-like, in the Metaxy between ideas and life; the Bard gives us many noble insights if we read him without making slavish assumptions about human nature.

Shakespeare backs tragic poetry against triumphal history. His ideal ruler is neither a victorious Hamlet nor a nihilistic fantastic wallowing in absurdity; *Antony and Cleopatra* urges us to choose sacrificial love over Pyrrhic victory. A polis affirming equality and linking Platonic Eros to Christ's gospel is the basis for the best commonwealth; here, instead of calling men doomed sinners, to be ruled like prodigal pigs, we see true beauty and find happiness in bringing out the best in each other. As Cleopatra saw, even the pagan gods envy the power of lovers to generously give of themselves, bringing the world beauty and happiness by this tragic and sacrificial but truly human activity. In short, *Antony and Cleopatra* points to the essence of Jesus' life and gospel. By rejecting misanthropic self-hatred, a condition all too easily abused by priests, and affirming the possibility of living generously and well on the earth, the play preserves Christian humanism, the true meaning of the Renaissance, and conveys it to a world still ruled by Rome's false gods: generation, greed and globalization.

Antony and Cleopatra looks to our time; the basic struggle is between fascism—a sinister simulacrum of the common good—and the commune.

Even as the corporate right relentlessly centralizes and consolidates power, the communal left splinters into liberal identity politics, preferring private pleasure and proclaiming personal pain to pursuing post-political power. Both sides deny and even denounce any notion of the common good. *Antony and Cleopatra* shows how it could be otherwise.